DATE

Psychotherapy

Psychotherapy

RALPH W. HEINE

Prentice-Hall, Inc., Englewood Cliffs, New Jersey

C–13–736801–1

P–13–736793–7

Library of Congress Catalog Card Number: 75–125087

Printed in the United States of America

Current Printing (last digit):
10 9 8 7 6 5 4 3 2 1

PRENTICE-HALL INTERNATIONAL, INC., London
PRENTICE-HALL OF AUSTRALIA, PTY. LTD., Sydney
PRENTICE-HALL OF CANADA, LTD., Toronto
PRENTICE-HALL OF INDIA PRIVATE LIMITED, New Delhi
PRENTICE-HALL OF JAPAN, INC., Tokyo

Preface

No one in the course of a lifetime altogether escapes troublesome personal conflicts and periods of emotional turmoil. Such upsets are usually self-limiting and quite manageable with the support and reassurance of friends or family members. However, as a society becomes increasingly urbanized and complex, many of its members are separated from familiar and dependable social groups that have served both as supports and as guides for living.

Such uprooted individuals and those in transit from one kind of life to another (among whom college students represent a sizable proportion) are both more prone to uncertainty and self-doubt and less likely to have trusted confidants readily available. It is out of this growing need for an institutionalized friend that the professional psychotherapist has come to be valued.

The practice of psychotherapy is by no means limited to clients with very severe personal conflicts or disabling symptoms. Most clients of psychotherapists are functioning reasonably well, but many have the uneasy feeling that they are not getting as much out of life as they should, or cannot define to their own satisfaction who they are and in what direction they should be going, and they therefore have great difficulty in assigning priorities to goals and values to personal relationships.

Thus, the psychotherapist has an important role in society, particularly for those individuals who have the greatest degree of freedom of choice. Yet there is serious question whether any psychotherapist has developed a theory and technique that can dependably cure an individual of problems that, to a considerable extent, are the product of stresses peculiar to life in contemporary society.

At the same time, a great deal of zeal and ingenuity has gone into devising therapeutic techniques resting on the assumption that an individual can be helped to alter his view of himself and others so that he can confidently master the normal range of problems he confronts in society. Moreover, a very large number of practitioners and clients continue to believe in the efficacy of individual psychotherapy. Thus, it is important for any informed person to have some familiarity with the theory and practice of psychological treatment of emotional problems, just as he should know about any other significant facet of living in modern times.

This book is directed to undergraduates in courses devoted to abnormal psychology or clinical methods, but it can also help any intelligent layman gain an understanding of psychotherapy as it is construed by a number of prominent schools that have grown up around the theory and practice of such outstanding men as Sigmund Freud, Carl Rogers, and B. F. Skinner, who was not himself a therapist but whose techniques are widely used to modify behavior. The intended tone of this book is one of benign skepticism, for, as Louis August Gottschalk and Arthur Henry Auerbach (1966) have said, "Everyone knows what psychotherapy is. But it is easier to write a plausible convincing book explaining the subject and the method than to prove a single assertion about it with any degree of scientific rigor." There is certainly no question about the importance of the goals of psychotherapy or about the sincerity of the collaborative efforts of practitioners and clients. There is, however, some question about the scientific standing of the theories and practices currently in use, and this fact should be held in mind by the reader as he considers the merits of each viewpoint.

Thus, it is not without cause that a very recent trend among troubled people, only briefly discussed in this book, is to seek companionship in groups that may be designated as therapeutic but are often conducted by the participants themselves, without a trained therapist. Moreover, in large metropolitan areas there has been a highly accelerated growth of open social gatherings for various age groups, computerized dating services, bars, nightclubs, resorts, pleasure cruises, and even apartment complexes catering to singles—services for lonely individuals of both sexes who lack dependable attachments to a community of friends and relatives. Some observers suggest that these group experiences will replace individual therapists as a source of guidance for many present and potential clients.

I would like to acknowledge with gratitude the assistance received from Elton McNeil who as Series Editor was responsible for my being invited to write the book, and from Richard Lazarus whose comments on the manuscript at various stages in its preparation were extremely useful.

Mrs. Betty Edwards, my secretary, deserves particular thanks for managing, in ways best known to herself, to type several drafts of the manuscript and to provide editorial assistance despite a heavy burden of other work.

Contents

Psychotherapy

The Nature of Psychotherapy

Psychotherapy can be seen either as a transparently simple phenomenon that everyone intuitively understands and has practiced, or as a confused, incredibly complex process well beyond the reach of current scientific understanding. Considered merely as a collective term for events that have a demonstrably salutary effect on one's state of mind, psychotherapy is readily comprehensible to everyone. In this sense of the term, the catalog of potentially psychotherapeutic human experiences is endless.

A partial list of positive experiences would include the following: (1) The large number of induced physiological changes that have a reflection in awareness as "pleasant," or at least as a transition from more to less unpleasant. The stimuli for such changes range from those that repair normal deficits (such as food, water, sexual orgasm, rest, temperature change, increased or decreased demands on the senses and the muscular systems) to drugs that produce a wide range of discernible effects (such as analgesics, soporifics, and psychedelics). (2) The even larger number of events that alter the state of well-being at the psychological level: achievements, avoidance of failure, exercise of skills and abilities, entertainment, and so on. (3) Events at the interpersonal or social group level: enhancement of social recognition, increased degree of acceptability to or belongingness in a valued group, or enhanced control over the range and type of one's social participation.

1

SELF-TREATMENT AND
PROFESSIONAL THERAPY

All human behavior is in one way or another concerned with manipulating the self or the environment to provide psychotherapy when it is needed, and, practically speaking, this is rather frequently. It is apparent that there is a significant degree of interpenetration between all three of the systems described—physiological and social events interact with the psychological system. Furthermore, almost no event in any one of the three systems can fail to have some influence on the other two. It is because of this that we have so much difficulty pinning down human behavior and conceptualizing the psychotherapeutic process.

A common discomfort—such as diffuse tension and vague uneasiness—could stem from physical or sensory fatigue, from a personal problem, or from unfavorable or disappointing behavior of others. In fact, these minor symptoms may be the products of dislocations in all three spheres. If the difficulty seems to have been initiated in one sphere, it is likely to be reflected quickly through the other two.

Treatment along physiological dimensions might consist of a sedative and rest; psychological treatment might involve engaging in some familiar diversion which is almost always satisfying, or seeking out acquaintances who are customarily friendly and reassuring. Such treatments may temporarily ease distress, but most recurrent, unpleasant circumstances that create tension and anxiety can neither be avoided nor rationally resolved. A mild, restitutive therapy is all one can really prescribe for himself. One is, in effect, saying, "I think I know what's bothering me, and I've done as much as I can to resolve it, but there's a residual carryover of tension I can dissolve by being especially nice to myself."

However, when we go beyond the normal symptomatology of everyday life to consider severe anxiety and tension, self-treatment may be ineffective and even dangerous: as the level of anxiety and tension increases, the capacity for accurate self-scrutiny is reduced—as is acuity in reading the behavior of others. In serious circumstances, the need for relief is so insistent that remedial efforts have a desperate quality that often accentuates the very problems one is trying to avoid. Thus, physiological interventions such as drugs, alcohol, or even sleep may temporarily relieve tension only to lead to the more serious problem of addiction. Drug-induced changes in physiological status can have a transient salutary effect on the psychological system in any one of several ways—such as permitting extravagant gratification without regard for social or personal consequences, pushing painfully difficult, unresolved conflicts out of consciousness, or permitting problem-solving in fantasy without regard for reality. The effects of such remedial efforts are, nevertheless, likely to be uniformly harmful, since the resultant altered behavior disrupt long-standing social patterns. Specialists in drug addiction, for example, have come to believe that physiological dependency is only one aspect of the problem. The addict becomes increasingly preoccupied with the process of finding a source of the drug, obtaining funds for it, and organizing the drug-taking rituals. Moreover, the addict is drawn into a social group tightly bound together by their mutual dependency and common status as outcasts. Thus, treatment is not merely a matter of detoxification, but also of providing alternative interests that are as all-consuming, and a social existence at least as gratifying.

There is, then, a point at which psychotherapy, to be effective, may have to be turned over to someone other than the suffering individual. Yet noting the limitations on self-help does not better define what psychotherapy is, and, given the current state of knowledge, we are not likely to arrive at such a definition. A simple report of what is done in the name of psychotherapy leads to a definition of psychotherapy as almost any kind of intervention in a patient's life that leads either to the patient's reporting a salutary effect on his state of mind or to an observer's noting some salutary change in the patient's behavior.

This is not to say that there are no characteristics that differentiate professional psychotherapists from would-be helpers among family members, friends, and associates. The psychotherapist has a *professional* as contrasted with a determined *personal* interest in his client; he has a *theory* and *practice* to guide him in his transactions with his client; and he usually has agreed to abide by a *code of ethics* that safeguards his client against exploitation.

Since it is often a rather poignant issue for clients whether or not their therapist has a *personal* interest in their problems, the meaning of the term in this context should be further explored. Friends and relatives have a personal interest in a client because what he does both reflects on them and affects their plans and level of self-esteem. Thus, for example, parents may have a personal interest in their son's therapy because his behavior is contrary to their standards of conduct and may embarrass them in their social group, even if it does not jeopardize their status. Parents often have very definite therapeutic goals for their children and usually want only one outcome—voluntary and convinced modification of behavior and beliefs in the direction of the social norms to which they ascribe. Friends may have a personal interest along similar lines, although their particular aspirations for the client may be quite different from those of his parents or spouse. In this sense, personal interest means a generalized, long-standing emotional attachment to the client, together with some fairly definite ideas about what behavior of his is or is not gratifying.

The psychotherapist's interest in his client is personal in that he cares very much how the individuals he treats meet their problems, and he genuinely hopes that they can use therapy to enhance their capacity for realistic self-gratification. But the therapist is not personally involved in supporting a particular set of solutions.

Many clients find it necessary to test their therapists, usually with attitudes or behaviors that have proved very provocative in relationships with parents, spouses, or close associates. When the therapist does not rise to the same bait, the client assumes that the therapist is indifferent to his problems. The problem of trust of a client in his therapist is central to any psychotherapeutic understanding, and one important aspect of trust is a belief in the genuineness of the therapist's interest. It is very difficult for many clients, even those rather sophisticated in the ways of psychotherapy, to accept the fact that a therapist can have a personal interest and yet remain calm in the face of disclosures that, in other contexts, usually produce alarm and anxiety.

PHYSIOLOGICAL, PSYCHOLOGICAL, AND INTERPERSONAL APPROACHES TO THERAPY

Just as an individual can treat himself by physiological, psychological, or social means, so can psychotherapists intervene along a number of parameters. Many professional mental health specialists argue that the therapist who prescribes rest, a vacation, a drug, or electroshock is not a *psycho*therapist. Some would make the same assertion regarding therapists who manipulate the social milieu. But if intervention along the physiological or social parameters has demonstrable influence in the psychological sphere, as relief of felt tensions, then, I would argue, it is *psycho*therapy. Man can usefully be viewed as comprising a physiochemical system, a psychological system, and a transacting "node" in a complex social network. These systems are closely integrated and interdependent. Eventually all therapists, whether termed psychotherapists or not, must take all three parameters into account if their work is to be brought within the scope of science.

Table 1.1 may help elucidate current conceptions of treatment. It does not properly reflect the complex relationships that exist between the

TABLE 1.1   MENTAL ILLNESS AND PSYCHOTHERAPY: CURRENT APPROACHES

Conception of Mental Illness	Diagnostic Procedure	Treatment
Biological		
Overload on central nervous system leads to permanent switching on of emergency reactions. Subjective experience is one of readiness for flight or fight for which there is no adequate response. Hence tension and anxiety which, in extreme cases, lead to freezing or uncontrollable rage reaction.	Essentially a medical history and a review of bodily systems with special attention to organs known to respond sensitively to changes in emotional status. Mental status examination and review of presenting complaints.	Psychotropic or sedative drugs and, occasionally, electroconvulsive shock. Rest and recreation. Treatment of secondary functional symptoms in organs. Brief supportive interviews.
Psychological		
Intrapsychic imbalance is created by failure of ego defenses to modulate instinctual impulses or superego demands. Subjective experience is one of tension and anxiety or, in extreme cases, depersonalization.	Psychological interviews supplemented by psychodiagnostic tests lead to a formulation regarding the probable experiences reactivated by contemporary stress.	Frequent individual interviews initially aimed at creating an atmosphere of trust within which the patient can dissolve rigid defenses and explore the impulses and conflicts which, outside of awareness, produced anxiety. When insight is achieved, "working through" of constructive alternatives to neurotic solutions can begin.
Interpersonal		
Fabric of roles and relationships is disrupted, with consequent threatened loss of identity. Hence tension and anxiety which, in extreme cases, become panic or withdrawal.	Systematic review of relationships with significant others— individuals and groups— with emphasis on recent changes in long-standing patterns of mutual dependency or group membership and social statuses and roles.	Parallel or conjoint treatment of family members or individual interviews designed to explore interpersonal relations in detail. In rehabilitative phase of severe mental illness, role-training for the patient and counseling with the family members and prospective employer are designed to expedite reentry into normal social life.

5

systems. It is a regrettable fact of current theory and practice that each of the three approaches has many articulate adherents, but each group asserts that it represents the whole pie instead of one piece of it. Consequently, we are constrained by the state of the field to consider as separate and distinct, theories and practices of psychotherapy which properly should be subsumed under a general theory of intervention into emotional and behavioral disorders.

The preponderance of evidence suggests that interventions along any of the three parameters discussed have roughly equal chances of producing symptomatic improvement (Koegler and Brill, 1967). This does not indicate that all therapies are identical in all or even most respects, but rather suggests that humans are far more complex than the theories developed to account for their behavior. Wittingly or unwittingly, people are able to absorb and make use of many kinds of help that seem to have little in common and may not even be intended as psychotherapeutic. Moreover, how a therapist offers his help may be more important than what he does. A pill can be administered in a matter of seconds in a manner that is more reassuring than an hour's interview. A seemingly casual exchange between a student and a teacher at a critical point in the student's life my be more therapeutic, although not defined as such, than a series of formal counseling sessions.

The skills and sensitivity of the therapist are difficult to define and measure reliably, but they are certainly more important than the particular techniques and theory he purports to use (Heine 1953; Draper 1965). Similarly, the receptivity of an individual to help, or his readiness to make changes in his life style, may have a great deal more to do with the amount of relief he gains than the particular kind of therapy he receives. Indeed, the research literature suggests that even patients on a waiting list can make improvements closely resembling those of patients who are treated (Frank 1959).

A MODEL OF PERSONALITY

The brief, all-purpose model of personality functioning that follows may help explain this seeming paradox and aid the reader in following the chapter on psychodiagnostic evaluation. The model will summarize some of the common elements in several of the most widely applied models of personality functioning. In the chapters on the various approaches to psychotherapy, there will be additional remarks on the particular theories held by representatives of various schools.

It is usually possible to describe and reliably classify sets of human characteristics even if the relationships among them cannot be explained. However, simple measurement and classification is hardly satisfying to the psychologist bent on making coherent sense of the behavior of the whole person. Indeed, all of us have some notions about how human characteristics, behaviors, and events fit together—about what is cause and what is effect in human affairs. It is clearly essential to social existence that we do have ideas about why people do what they do and that we have reasonably well-developed notions about the consistency of particular patterns of behavior. Utter chaos would follow from a total or even a relative lack of predictability of human behavior.

Although everyone must have theory of human behavior generated out of his life experience, few people are able to articulate their theory in any detail. If asked, "Why does X do Y?" they would be likely to respond, "because it is the custom," or "it's his job to do Y," or, "because X is that kind of person," or (in more intimate transactions), perhaps, "because X knows that if he does not do Y, I will not do Z." In general, our expectations about behavior are based on role requirements, exchange principles, and commonly understood opportunity and reward structures. These are carefully and sometimes painfully learned as we grow up. However, our integration into our social milieu is generally so complete that our responses are virtually automatic, and in that sense unconscious.

Nevertheless, there are enough surprises, miscalculations, disappointments, and uncertainties to make us keenly aware of the existence of individual differences and of the highly probabilistic (as contrasted with fully determined) nature of our social existence. There are, indeed, large areas of common social and personal experience on which we can build predictions, but these common experiences are variously interpreted and reacted to by various individuals.

The attempt to make sense of what is not completely predictable by reference to role, custom, and experience has led theorists to create an imaginary organ (a hypothetical construct) called *personality*. The postulation that everyone has such an organ or system that receives and organizes experience and governs behavior of all kinds makes it possible to build alternative models of human behavior.

It should be made clear that there is no such thing as a personality. To put it another way, a personality can be conceptualized in whatever way helps the theoretician, research, or clinician in his effort to understand the complex relationships among bits of observed behaviors. Yet to the layman and scientist alike, one's self-awareness, one's planfulness, one's capacity for experiencing pain and pleasure, and one's acute sensitivity to his level of well-being seem to be compelling evidence of an integrated, almost real entity which is as much a part of being alive as any other organ.

In all sciences there are theories or models that, although imperfect, serve to stimulate further discovery and investigation. There is rarely as much intuitive support for such concepts as there is for the assumption that all of us have a personality. Everyone is not only convinced that he has a personality, he also believes that he is reasonably well informed about its characteristics. This presents a problem when the proponents of various personality theories become convinced that the hypotheses they advance are literally true, rather than convenient but contrived metaphors for organizing their observations of human behavior.

There are many competing theories of personality. Our principal need here is to abstract from them certain widely held conceptions of the functioning of personality. We need to consider the essentials of the personality of man as construed by many theorists before we can comprehend the nature of diagnostic and treatment schemes in current use.

Most contemporary theories of personality are what is termed *dynamic*. This implies that behavior—composed of thoughts, feelings, and actions—is always the resultant of several competing forces contesting for expression in each individual. Just what these forces are and how they interact is the subject of continuing and often bitter controversy among theorists. The issue cannot be easily settled by weighing the demonstrated scientific merit of one theory against another. Several theories may explain observed behavior equally well (or equally poorly), and certainly all contain a welter of speculation about events that are either unobservable or not easily subjected to systematic investigation.

Personality theorists, like other observant people, have noted that virtually all people exhibit several kinds of behavior. Most people, children and adults alike, go through rather mundane cycles of sleeping, working, and playing in reasonable conformity with the norms of the larger society or the subculture in which they live. They give every appearance of setting about planfully, with regard for what is realistically available to them, to enhance their well-being, whether alone or in collaboration with others.

But a closer scrutiny reveals that, woven into this fabric of customary self-enhancing behavior, are many acts that suggest internal restraints not clearly dictated by limitations imposed by the outside world. Some of these acts occasionally seem unnecessarily self-punitive and self-defeating. And some portion of human behavior seems poorly controlled, strongly emotional, and in some instances destructive and disruptive both to the individual's best interests and to the well-being of those about him.

Many theorists—particularly those concerned with psychotherapy— have hypothesized that the organ of personality is best described as being comprised of at least three interacting systems. In function, these parts may frequently be antagonistic to each other, so that what emerges as observable behavior is a compromise among several possible alternatives.

The Executive Part

One part of the self or personality, it has been conjectured, carrys out an executive function: it carefully appraises reality, weighs all reasonable alternative actions, and sets in motion those sequences of behavior that will most assure personal gratification, while neutralizing or minimizing threats to the self and the sought gratification. It is evident that no two people make identical appraisals of reality, or view precisely the same array of actions and accomplishments as gratifying. Indeed, a number of choices is available to any individual at ony one moment.

Since many gratifications depend upon collaborative relationships between two or more people, the tasks of the executive part of the personality are both complex and demanding. Ideal functioning demands a staggering number of minute-by-minute appraisals of what is taking place internally and in the external world, and computer-like calculation of the probabilities involved in the various available courses of action. Moreover, the executive part of the self is frequently required to redeploy energy and alter decisions to meet the tactics employed by others, and to establish a strategy sufficiently flexible to meet changing situations.

Suffice it to say that no one comes close to the ideal of perpetually alert, perfect functioning. If the executive part of the personality were to give attention to all internal and external stimuli, it would be chronically overloaded. It is the manner in which this constant threat of overload is handled that contributes in large measure to observable and sometimes measurable individual differences. The enormously complex job of the executive part of personality is further complicated by the intrusive demands of the other parts of the self which, like powerful dissident minorities in a legislature, constantly urge the executive branch to actions that may be impractical and at odds with the quest for optimal satisfaction and gratification.

The Conscience

Among theorists, there is considerable controversy over what the capacities and functions of the other two parts of the personality are. One of the parts seems to be the repository of a set of arbitrary, often irksome rules for living which the executive must take into account in planning strategies. These rules do not conform to reality demands, since they seem to be fixed and immutable even when the real situation changes. The executive may try to ignore them, but it does so at the risk of contaminating the gratification achieved—which may be guilt laden and strangely unsatisfying. Gratification achieved at the expense of violating these rules seems to be compromised by unpleasant feelings, feelings quite like those experienced when one is sternly admonished by persons important to one's well-being, such as parents or valued friends. Since the executive part of the personality has the responsibility of taking into account a whole series of internal and external factors in maximizing well-being, it must forego those behaviors prohibited by these arbitrary rules, or it must go to great lengths to disguise such undertakings so they seem justified, reasonable, and acceptable.

Just as the executive part of the personality is what most of us think of as being our most familiar, planful self, this second part is what in ordinary language is usually referred to as the conscience. At its best, it is a useful, automatic guide to socially condoned decisions and actions in situations too complex for the executive to compute quickly and accurately; at its worst it is a nagging, punitive force which gives every appearance of trying to make the task of the executive impossible.

The Third Part and the
Dynamics of Disfunction

Theorists have had most difficulty conceptualizing the third part of the organ of personality, for this part has been identified as the source of the most contradictory behaviors in man. Where the executive part undertakes planful, logical, well-modulated, self-enhancing behavior, the third part dictates alogical, planless, rude, impulsive, and sometimes unrestrainedly destructive behavior. Some theorists believe that it is exactly these uninhibited, unrestrained impulses that are the source of the most original and creative parts of thought and action. Yet the executive part of the self is usually too aware of all the pitfalls and dangers of chance-taking and characteristically modulates, redirects, and disguises both the creative and destructive impulses.

Since the functions of the executive self are clearly evident, and the utility of conscience in most of its manifestations seems to make sense as a guide to social acceptability, theorists usually have no difficulty accounting for the development of these functions. Unfortunately, the unregenerate third part of the personality has not been explored with qual vigor. Most commonly, it is simply viewed as instinctual—as a primitive remnant of an early stage in the evolutionary development of man. It is viewed as the source of behavior that was once, perhaps, useful for survival, but now is a perpetual threat to civilized living—a primitive "personality" which is now encapsulated and controlled with difficulty. Yet, many theorists believe that this system is at the same time a prime source of energy and inspiration for the highly socialized, self-aware executive and the rule-observing conscience.

While this is a plausible assumption, the work of naturalists and ethologists shows that, taken species by species, animals are typically not beastly toward one another, nor are they, within the limits of their endowment, alogical, irrational, or self-destructive. Although one would not attribute to animals all the features of human personality (because animals lack the reflective self-awareness that comes with the ability to use language), the patterned behavior of animals reflects something very much like human planfulness, playfulness, and, if not conscience, at least something closely resembling what we term forebearance, loyalty, helpfulness, and so on. Although there are rogues among animals who may, on rare occasions, wantonly attack members of their own species, only man systematically and ruthlessly decimates his own kind, and only man's sexual appetite knows no season and is frequently expressed in ways errant from the typical heterosexual genital contact of "lower" mammals. These differences raise a serious question as to whether the characterisitics associated with the dark, impulse-ridden part of the personality should properly be viewed as an animal-like inheritance from a primitive ancestor, a biological base on which a highly articulated social life has been constructed.

Whether animal-like or not, this part of personality is said to be the source of impulses that, because they are inconsistent with life as conducted in highly organized social groups, must be kept under firm control. To this task, the executive part of the self must presumably devote a great deal of energy and a high level of vigilance. Indeed, the degree of danger from these potentially destructive aggressive and sexual acts is deemed to be so great that the executive, like the mythical Perseus in his encounter with the Gorgon, Medusa, cannot look directly at them but must wait for a signal, in the form of anxiety, that something is amiss. The executive then introduces emergency defenses to stem the rising tide of uneasiness.

Another view of this part of the personality is that it is not comprised of inherited, perverse tendencies but is a kind of repository of significant (and frightening) failures of the executive self during its early development, when its capacity for calculating the best resolution of a complex situation was limited by inexperience. Such failures (usually early childhood acts, with aggressive or sexual implications, that were severely punished or created visible alarm and intense anxiety in adults) cannot be repeated and worked through to more successful conclusions, and they would best be forgotten. But because they can neither be forgotten nor replayed and more effectively resolved in later life, they are continuing threats to the smooth operation of the executive part of the self—rather like a remote, warlike, primitive tribe in an otherwise developed nation. They are largely forgotten but occasionally break out of their reservation and must be quelled. The signal that a serious forgotten error is about to reappear is anxiety, and the responding posture of the executive is tense, defensive alertness.

A third version of how impulsive, antisocial behavior in humans should be understood is that such actions are neither an inherited supply of socially unacceptable impulses, nor a heavily guarded repository of errors committed when young, but simply an indication of gross executive error. That is, the executive, when greatly overtaxed, allocates energy to highly implausible and inappropriate solutions to pressing problems. The theory is that the executive routinely examines unrealistic and antisocial problem solutions along with more plausible and accepted ones. Since, almost without exception, impulsive, destructive, or antisocial solutions tend to be relatively simple and direct, the overtaxed executive resorts to these simple solutions to ease overloads.

In this view, socially uncondoned behavior occurs under two rather different circumstances. An individual who has rarely received instruction or rewards (by way of attention, affection, approbation, and, above all, success) for achieving gratification in ways that take account of the needs and feelings of others clearly cannot be expected to exercise the executive function in the same way as an individual who gratifys his needs only when they are modulated by various proscriptions and rules of conduct which have been rewarded by the favorable attention of significant adults. This does not imply that early experience produces fundamentally different types of people, but rather that the seeking of gratification by crude, direct means without regard for consequences occurs more frequently in the lives of individuals for whom the only early models of problem-solving were persons who themselves often sought direct and immediate means of achieving gratification.

A second case in which socially uncondoned behavior occurs is during certain life circumstances that evoke impulsive, violent behavior in almost anyone. However, such behavior usually occurs late in the array of availble alternatives, especially when one's entire life has been devoted to estraint as a tactic. Impulsive behavior occurs relatively easily when one 1as learned to seize what is immediately gratifying first and question what >ne has done later, if one questions it at all.

HUMAN BEHAVIOR AS AN EMERGENT SYSTEM

Differences in viewpoints about the development of the three aspects of personality functioning have considerable significance for the theory and practice of psychotherapy and for psychodiagnostic formulations. We cannot here try to give a complete description of the exquisitely complicated proceedings that, taken together, comprise the thoughts and behavior of a fully functioning human individual. Nor do we wish to give an exposition of personality theory or metapsychology as such. Rather, we will set ourselves the more limited task of trying to describe some of the sources of overload of the executive function.

There is no question that humans do engage in the three kinds of behavior described earlier. Nor does it seem disputable that emotional and behavioral disturbances can be construed as reflections of a failure of the executive function. What is questionable is the notion that failures due to an overload on the capacity of an individual to resolve problems of living are caused, in any direct one-to-one relationship, either by internal impulses or arbitrary constraints of conscience or by external stimuli such as demands of the social environment. The notions of cause and effect that we conventionally apply to behavior are no more than convenient fictions; we like to assign causes to human behavior in the interests of maintaining an illusion of understanding. Moreover, many of us are inclined to use a simple, mechanistic model in analyzing the causes of human behavior.

The probable truth of the matter is that there are no causes of human behavior in the usual sense in which this term is used. This is not to say that human events "just happen."

Sophisticated environmental scientists no longer ask what causes air pollution or the decay of cities or the extinction of species of animals; political scientists do not ask what causes revolutions or the emergence of nationalism; economists do not try to identify causes of depressions. Rather, taking the decay of the inner core of large metropolises as an example, urban specialists now describe major cities as complex systems of forces—physical, economic, political, social, and psychological—all of which interact with each other with some structure but constant flux. I is possible to give a partial description of a city at two points in time anc to note differences between point A and point B. One such difference might be the physical deterioration of large areas of human dwellings Given a number of such differences in a time sequence, it may also be pos- sible to make some judgment about the viability of the system and give some crude estimates of what could be done to modify it. But it is not pos- sible to isolate a cause of any particular condition nor to predict accurately the effect of any particular intervention. Humans are not cities or lakes or economies, but they too are systems rather than automata, and their behavior is, similarly, not so much caused as emergent.

Humans are reactive and resourceful under stress and they have that gift of inestimable value, the capacity for self-reflection. Not surprisingly, then, one of our treasured beliefs is that we are responsible for our be- havior. If we accomplish socially valued things, we are inclined to be self- congratulatory; if we commit socially disapproved acts, we are inclined to feel ashamed and guilty, or at least angry if apprehended. But it may be that we can no longer accept the simple notion of individual responsi- bility for behavior.

Just as many observers are now reluctant to say that city slums are caused by malicious landlords or by the inmigration of Southern Blacks, so we have come to believe that human behavior is emergent from a highly complex system of forces. According to this view, we cannot change behavior patterns by changing child care alone, by modifying education alone, by enhancing economic well-being alone, by improving law enforcement alone, by speeding political change alone, or by offering psychotherapy, in all its forms, alone. All these influences on behavior must be modified together, according to patterns we are far short of comprehending. The one thing we are reasonably certain of is that man, like the natural world of which he is a part, is lawful, not in the legal but in the scientific sense of the term.

The physiochemical-psychological-social entity that is the human individual is a system in which every part is in communication with every other part. Thus, at the interface between the person and his social environment there is always transaction. The individual reacts to and evokes stimulation in a perpetual cycle circumscribed only by the range he can tolerate. Transactions with the social environment are listed first because, in the most profound sense, man is a social animal, and *all* of his psychological activity is, in the final analysis, in the service of maintaining himself in a tolerable social climate. The sum total of activities devoted to defining and maintaining the ndividual in his social system is what we refer to as personality. The individual makes certain demands on his social microcosm, and the people comprising it make certain demands upon him. Ideally, a kind of fluctuating, steady state is achieved in which there is never exact parity of exchange and never wide discrepancy. From the point of view of the individual, there are periods of deliberate action and periods of apparent inaction. At times of apparent inaction, there is, nevertheless, activity in the sense of planning future action or a shift of a particular set of transactions to a level of phantasy. Deliberate action can be at varying levels of intensity and directionality. All these events are modulated by social stimuli, which are themselves modulated by the reaction to them. It is obvious that, visualized in this manner, assigning a *cause* to a breakdown in the exchange pattern is virtually impossible; rather, a failure *emerges* from the ebb and flow of transactions.

FAILURE OF THE SYSTEM

How does the system get out of kilter? How does a situation of overload on the executive function of the personality occur? If there were a completely free market on transactions, system failures would occur far less frequently than they do. Unfortunately, many arbitrary restraints and demands serve to complicate parity in exchanges between the system which is the individual human and his social environment.

One can easily describe the kind of constraints that are part of everyone's experience. As already noted, there are certain behaviors which, on an ethical or moral basis, we ought to engage in and others we ought not, irrespective of other conditions. Our behavior is organized into bundles called roles—jobs, etiquettes, duties, and so on which, once learned and seriously undertaken, cannot be easily disassembled. One feels he ought perform the aggregate of behaviors related to these socially defined and sanctioned functions whether he feels like it or not. The need to perform is experienced as an internal push powerfully reinforced by the social environment which, sometimes subtly, sometimes vigorously, nudges the recalcitrant into line. A stark example is the transformation of the draftee into a soldier. Adopting the roles and responsibilities of a G.I. may be the last thing a draftee has in mind. Yet, once the gates of the training camp close behind him, he is subjected to almost irresistible pressures to perform soldierly functions. Moreover, once he is socialized into the role he may be put in the position of carrying out acts completely contrary to his prior values, beliefs, and practices. In ways less poignant but just as inexorable all of us are com mitted by our place in the social order to tasks, confrontations, an conflicts often more demanding of our resources than we would prefe However, the alternative of disengagement is usually even more trying since we then suffer from a stimulus hunger that is hard to satisfy in ac ceptable ways.

All subsystems in the larger system are perpetually in motion and interacting with each other. That is, the environment is stimulating modifications in interpersonal behavior, which are in turn modifying the social environment, which is then making somewhat different demands for behavior. Meanwhile, within the individual, there are communications between the physiochemical substrate and the area of executive function, and communications between the executive and the areas labeled *conscience* and *impulse*. The executive, moreover, alternates between thinking planfully and thinking playfully, as in fantasy.

Rather than indicating chaotic activity, this ceaseless flow of energy marks the fluctuating, steady state of the individual's transactions with his social environment. An abrupt change anywhere in the system radiates across the network (although an abrupt change is usually merely a noticeable consequence of a number of smaller changes) and requires adjustment in all sectors. If the adjustment cannot be made, the individual experiences increasing tension and discomfort, because permissable limits of stimulation have been exceeded.

This can come about when the level of physical energy falls (because of illness or advancing age, for example) without a corresponding reduction in energy expedition in the social sphere; when a miscalculation occurs and a new role or status responsibility proves to be unexpectedly demanding; when a drastic change in status occurs; when an impulse is acted upon in such a way that the demand characteristics of the social environment are radically altered; and in many similar circumstances. These circumstances can be altered to effect a return of the person-environment system to a steady state. A physician may order a sick person to reduce his work load; a new role may gain social approbation to the point of modifying the level of available energy; an impulse may be disowned and the characteristics of the social environment normalized, or the impulse may prove so gratifying that major changes in other activities are made to accommodate to its expression.

All of the first kinds of changes are tension-producing, while all the second are therapeutic, although no psychotherapist as such is involved. The changes are not fortuitous, however; they are inherent in a complex, reactive system.

Overload of the Executive

Under ideal circumstances, the executive part of personality maintains a constant, careful, reasonably accurate self-surveillance so as to make any adjustments dictated by perceived realities of the external environment and internal needs or wishes. The ideal task of the executive is impossible, and it must therefore take certain risks in the interests of work simplification. These risks most often have to do with attributing to relationships and to personal sentiments a stability which, in fact, is unwarranted. The simple fact is that most humans, of necessity, make some long-term commitments to other people, to lines of action, and to social institutions on the basis of a premise that is demonstrably incorrect: that nothing about the circumstances that made the commitment initially plausible will change significantly over time and that no important commitment will ever be in conflict with any other commitment in the future.

If the executive is really to function effectively it must either anticipate probable changes over the long run or establish a reserve of disposable energy to handle unpredictable contingencies. And the very high frequency with which humans engage in extravagant, personally costly behavior designed only to escape onerous commitments that seemed reasonable when made is testimony to the frailty of man's self-awareness and planfulness (see Pratt and Tooley, 1964).

Humans frequently make contracts they cannot live up to; and they frequently make contracts in direct conflict with each other. One example is the student who flunks out of college. Let us assume that only a very small proportion of students enter college with the intention of flunking out. Since a substantial proportion of entering freshmen never become sophomores, much less graduates, they must violate a contract with themselves, and perhaps with their parents, which might be stated, "I promise to devote all the time and energy to my coursework necessary to achieve passing grades." In failing to live up to this promise, students experience intense anxiety and depression, to say nothing of guilt toward parents and shame in the presence of more successful classmates.

How does the contract become eroded? Clearly, when a large number of unanticipated or only partially anticipated contingencies arise. The failing student will say, "Sure, I committed myself to spending the time on my studies necessary to pass but I didn't realize how *much* time this meant. And I didn't agree to give up dating, bull sessions with friends, and other attractive campus activities."

Having violated the contract, the student must then find means o renegotiating, or look for an escape clause. For example, he may suddenly realize that his courses are irrelevant, his instructors incompe tent, and his coursework far less involving than it had been painted. His contract violation is now comprehensible because he sees himself as having been taken in by spurious promises. He may now establish a new contract with himself to seek a "valid" education in the nonacademic world.

Another conspicuous example of such contractual difficulties is marital relationships. These are, of course, based on both legal and personal contracts, which may or may not be compatible. More than one in every three marriages in this country are legally dissolved, many before they have really become established. Again, it seems unlikely that any substantial number of marriages are consummated with either or both partners contemplating divorce. Nevertheless, each partner enters the relationship with a set of (largely unspoken and perhaps unwitting) demands he expects to make on the other, some negotiable and some non-negotiable. Each partner also enters with promises to himself regarding his comportment. At the same time, each partner has a set of contracts with a variety of other people—friends, relatives, employers—some of which are in direct conflict with those made to the marriage partner. Often before the bridal bouquet is wilted renegotiations begin, with a welter of "You didn't tell me that's . . .," "We clearly agreed that's . . .," "If I had only known's . . .," "If —— is more important to you than I am's . . .," and so on. Marriages that survive the renegotiations, however tension-producing, do succeed, and new contracts are established. Some of the terms may actually become explicit ("We'll join your family on Thanksgiving and mine on Christmas."), but most remain unspoken yet mutually understood. With each major stress—the arrival of children, a prospective move to a different city, illness, acute financial difficulties (or unexpected affluence)—there may be further renegotiations which stimulate anxiety and may degenerate into tension-ridden quarrels and divorce.

When one considers the vast and complicated legal apparatus that has had to be established to resolve such conflicts between impersonal institutions that are supposed to be entirely rational in the disposition of their affairs, it is scarcely surprising that individual humans often find themselves in deep trouble around matters of "contract violation." Not the least of the difficulty, as we have indicated, stems from the fact that most human commitments not only are not stated on paper in precise legal language but are never even verbalized!

Nevertheless, what humans do when caught in a contract violation is not different in principle from what business firms or governments do: unless they decide to skip out, they try to renegotiate the terms. Indeed, it is not far fetched to conceptualize the human condition as an endless and often tedious process of trying to live up to, demand fulfillment of, or renegotiate contracts with oneself or with significant others. What makes the process painfully complicated is that many of the crucial "facts" are not available to conscious scrutiny. Any doubts on this score can be settled by observing highly emotional and often confusing arguments between two or more persons. To those with experience in mediating quarrels, it is abundantly clear that what is at issue are not matters of fact but charges and counter-charges around presumed violations of agreements. The so-called facts in human affairs are always warped by the network of emotionally toned expectations, promises, judgments, and disappointments in which they are embedded.

Given this view of the problems faced by the executive part of the self, we have a better basis for understanding waiting-list or placebo cures. A great many, usually covert, renegotiations of contracts with significant others are undertaken both as a prelude to and as a consequence of a decision to seek outside intervention.

It is no easier to present schematically what happens when the executive copes with an overload than it is to try to draw a comprehensive diagram of the myriad biochemical consequences of simple fatigue. Mainly, this is because the formal syntax of our language forces us to describe complex events in a series of units that depict one facet at a time. The results can only be additive and can only imperfectly reflect the simultaneous character of psychological systems. Nevertheless, it is worthwhile to attempt to describe an individual's recovery while on a waiting list as a prelude to better understanding the various formal psychotherapies.

A Case History

The contrived but typical case history that follows is paradigmatic of the interplay of forces at work when an individual experiences an emotional disorder. It underlines the fact that the psychotherapist does not provide a specific remedy, but rather merely serves as an additional element in a complex, ongoing process. He draws attention to selective aspects of the process by encouraging its candid exploration and by providing the client with a way of looking at his experience that ties it

together and makes it seem more comprehensible. Psychotherapy is no
comparable to antibiotic treatment by an internist or to surgical opera
tions. The psychotherapist is drawn into the complex processing of affec
tive, cognitive, and sensory information by another person. But the erro
in the process may correct itself without him, or it may never be corrected
despite the therapist's best efforts.

Let us imagine a man in his early forties who is married, has two
teenage children, and is employed in the middle management of a
large company. For convenience we will assume that he can tolerate
100 units of stress—internally and environmentally generated—before
he is "overloaded." In examining his potential for tolerance of stress we
must take into account this normal load-bearing capacity as well as the
resilience of his environment.

Under ordinary conditions, our subject is geared for an average stress
of 80 units, and he tries to conduct his affairs at home and at work so as
to maintain a range of stress somewhere between 75 and 85 units. At
this level he feels comfortable. This state of relative well-being, however,
does not preclude his regularly scrutinizing his private uncertainties and
fears and testing the degree of confirmation or disconfirmation of them
he finds in his social environment. For example, he may state that his
job is "okay" and qualify this only by mentioning that it has both satisfying and unsatisfying features. Privately, he may sometimes have serious
doubts that he should have taken the job in the first place, fear that he
is not making normal progress, or that he is not well liked, respected, or
adequate to the job's demands. If these doubts are not confirmed, they
remain neutral and do not cause additional stress. Yet it is perfectly
possible to receive from superiors or colleagues intentional or accidental
messages that seem to confirm the validity of such doubts. Moreover, our
subject's past experience may have created areas of vulnerability that
lead him to overreact to some social cues and not to others. Doubts
thus nourished command a great deal of attention from the executive
part of the self, thereby diminishing its capacity to cope with more
routine problems.

Let us say that our subject's level of stress at this point stands at 90.
Outside of our subject's awareness lie some life-long feelings about adequacy and inadequacy acquired in childhood and no longer susceptible
to confirmation or disconfirmation by current information. These somewhat uncanny feelings, stemming from long-forgotten relationships,
may emerge unbidden to interfere at the very moment the executive
part of the self is trying desperately to handle growing doubts and
routine demands for efficient job performance. At first, our victim may

ry to cope with reality problems at a level of fantasy. He may entertain
leeting thoughts of omnipotence. These may be replaced by feelings, also
at a level of fantasy, of abject helplessness. These temporary extremes
of unrealistic thought, which represent self-images generated in childhood, are intensely anxiety-provoking and must be sternly suppressed by
the now hard-pressed executive. Consequently, the stress level now
stands at 95.

Meanwhile, because our subject is under increased stress, his capacity
to cope effectively with the routine demands of family life is lowered.
His wife notes his increasing tension and, in an attempt to be helpful,
asks what is bothering him. He mumbles vaguely that there is some
transient difficulty at work. His wife may realize that, like everyone
else, her husband has ups and downs which are of no lasting consequence,
and she may be mildly reassuring. She may also resolve to defer any
unusual demands she may be contemplating until her husband's psychological status is improved.

However, the subject's wife may already be troubled by his lack of
achievement. He may have for some time failed to live up to an implicit
commitment she required of him at the time of their marriage, but never
overtly told him about—to provide a certain status and level of security
within a certain reasonable period of time. She may for some time have
had doubts about their marriage, doubts that have preoccupied her and
that prevent her from seeing accurately the dimensions of his current
upset. Thus she may be made anxious by his casual report of trouble at
work, launch into a not-so-subtle criticism of his judgment in having
taken the job in the first place, and voice her doubts that he will ever
achieve what she expected of him. Her doubts and anxieties reinforce his
own, and he is confronted for the first time with an acute awareness that
he has failed to live up to the expectations of his wife. The ensuing fear
that she might leave him and the sense of guilt about his lack of accomplishment make him angry as well as awakening his own ambivalent
feelings about the marriage.

His load of stress now stands at 110—well above his level of tolerance
—and he experiences an increasingly severe, diffuse tension and anxiety.
From this point on his discomfort increases because his executive part
is so preoccupied both with worry about the future and reassessment of
the past that he begins to make hasty, poorly thought-out decisions. His
work, in fact, deteriorates and draws accurate negative criticism. The
spiral picks up speed, and his relationships with his wife and children
become increasingly troubled as he allows irritation generated at his
office to be displaced onto members of his family. At some point in this

period of exacerbation, his high level of stress may contribute to th
development of a series of psychogenic physical symptoms—headaches
stomach complaints, backaches, or irregularities of heartbeat. Ordinarily
he would give only casual attention to these aches and pains; now he may
seize on his physical distress as an explanation of his inefficiency at work
and deteriorating relationships at home.

Shortly, his symptoms, since he is now attracting public attention to
them, set in motion a number of changes in his social environment. His
superiors and his colleagues at work take note of his illness and in ways
both subtle and overt moderate the expectations and demands they make
of him. His wife reexamines her aspirations (which are dependent on
her husband's achievements) and renegotiates with herself the various
contracts she has with him. She may reluctantly but inevitably start to
play the role of a woman whose spouse is ill. She may, as the situation
apparently requires, adjust the cuisine, be more diligent about certain
additional household duties, admonish the children to "let Daddy rest,"
and graciously accept the sympathy of others who admire her persever-
ance in the face of adversity.

Thus, in the course of a few weeks, the external stress on our subject
is slowly reduced and his doubts are pushed aside by the imperative
demands of his illness. As a sick man he has a further obligation—to seek
treatment. This he will do after a decent interval of visible suffering, a
sincere effort at self-treatment with patent medicines, and regular dis-
claimers that his physician will have any answer for his complex array
of symptoms. Having established himself as someone who is suffering
physically (a condition that automatically commands sympathy, concern,
and special privilege), he seeks to consolidate his role of a man who is
ailing with professional validation. His physician orders a series of uncomfortable diagnostic tests that require an extended period of assessment of his condition. The subject's employer, colleagues, and family are
interested witnesses through each step of the procedure. Each facet of
the diagnostic and therapeutic effort is scrutinized in detail and described
on request.

From this point on, the process can take any one of several turns:
(1) The new balance of forces established by the illness can be stabilized
to produce a person permanently in delicate health. (2) Our subject can
gingerly test the possibility of recovering his health by probing to see
if what is expected of him has been substantially and permanently reduced. If the level of business, social, and personal demands on him are
lessened, he can safely return to something close to his normal level of
functioning. (3) His physician, having come up empty-handed medically,
may recommend a psychiatric approach to the treatment of his illness.

*f*is doctor may reluctantly refer him to a psychiatric outpatient clinic *w*here he is interviewed briefly and put on the waiting list. This unforeseen outcome presents our subject with a new set of cir-*c*umstances to deal with. Having made meaningful gains in reducing *h*is stress to a tolerable level, he would prefer to have the physical mani-*f*estations validated, so he can keep the internal and interpersonal sources *o*f stress a private matter. Like most people, he views with some alarm *t*he transformation of his apparent medical problem into a psychiatric *i*ssue. The most earnest efforts of national, regional, and local mental *h*ealth associations have failed to convince him that psychiatric illness has no more stigma attached to it than any other disorder. For him, there remains a wide psychological gulf between the notion, "your stomach is not functioning well," and the notion, "*you* are not functioning well." The latter is clearly judged by all but the most sophisticated patients to be a personal indictment.

One can certainly predict that our subject will be of two minds about his physician's recommendation. If the psychiatric referral is carefully and competently developed over time, he may experience some degree of relief that his real problems can at last be revealed. He may anticipate that the therapist could finally help him gain a relative degree of freedom from future discomfort. If, however, the referral is abruptly and inexpertly handled, he may recoil from the recommendation—particularly since he has already obtained some relief from the pressures that first made him anxious. He may dutifully accept the referral in order to maintain an image of his physician as rational and trustworthy, but he may be relieved at assignment to a waiting list rather than being swept into confrontation with immediate treatment. In this limited sense, he is actually cured before he accepts the referral to psychiatry. And it should be no surprise if, when asked about his status after a period of months, he reports that he is feeling better and that his symptoms have disappeared.

This case history illustrates several key points about psychotherapy: (1) What makes man human is having been reared in intimate association with other humans and the continuing, imperative need to remain in some kind of highly articulated social system. (2) As a consequence of this inescapable dependency on others, man spends a large part of his time communicating with others, replaying past communications, or rehearsing future interchanges. Ideally, perhaps, all communication should be syntactic—direct, explicit, and accurate. In fact, man learns from childhood that many important messages can be communicated only in a disguised form. (3) Symptoms represent one device for communicating without verbalization.

SYMPTOMATOLOGY AND DIAGNOSI*

All symptoms have in common this characteristic of communication with-out articulation. Symptoms are never developed exclusively to restore intrapsychic equilibrium; they always are in part directed at influencing significant people in the patient's life. The difficulty with symptoms as a means of communication is that, while they frequently speak loudly and attract attention, they seldom speak clearly and comprehensibly. People closely related to a patient always make some response to a symptom, but the response may not be the one sought. Very poignant examples of inappropriate responses to symptoms can be found in the literature on suicide; crys for help in the form of visible depression and anxiety, coupled with broad hints of self-destruction, are often met with recrimination rather than comprehension and assistance.

The point is that symptoms are not isolated, unintelligible aberrations. They are, rather, behaviors that are integral parts of a complex, inter-personal and intrapsychic process. That we cannot at this stage in our research or psychotherapy accurately trace these relationships should not deter us from aiming at such comprehensive understanding as our goal.

Meanwhile, we would do well not to depreciate past theories that calculatedly examine only certain limited phenomena while completely ignoring others. If we dismiss such efforts summarily, we will be without theory, for there is currently no comprehensive theory, even in broad and incomplete outline. We can make some use of the many contemporary approaches to psychotherapy. That they are not complete and exact is unfortunate, but no cause for rejection of all that we have accomplished to date. Our tools for capturing even some part of the ongoing, complex process of personality functioning—clinical evaluation of clients with psychodiagnostic tests—are far from adequate. Procedures for psycho-logical assessment try to categorize what cannot be categorized at all. They take a limited sample of the client's functioning, usually with only casual regard for the complex social context in which this functioning is occurring. But our successes and failures are clearly documented and form a platform for further investigation.

Psychodiagnostic Testing and Evaluation for Psychotherapy

2

Medical diagnosis should precede treatment. Many diseases produce superficially similar symptoms, and improper treatment may not only do little good, but it could be deadly. Moreover, it is important to know whether treatment is urgently required or merely elective.

While the custom of evaluating applicants for psychotherapy prior to treatment may have its origin in the conventions of medical practice, it actually has rather different objectives. Psychotherapy, in most circumstances, is a benign form of treatment. If it does not always cure, it almost never kills. Moreover, it is a nonspecific form of treatment: there is relatively little matching of symptoms with specific therapeutic procedures. The individual practitioner is inclined to use his particular brand of psychotherapy regardless of the presenting problem.

GOALS OF EVALUATION

Paradoxically, the more obviously disturbed a patient is, the less is the likelihood he will be offered psychotherapy, at least as an outpatient. Thus, perhaps the primary objective of evaluation is to make an assessment of the client's treatability. In practical terms this means that the therapist or diagnostician tries to determine (1) whether the applicant can grasp the objectives and procedures of psychotherapy and participate in them collaboratively; and (2) whether the prospective client can comport

25

himself so as to create no emergencies and require no extraordinary services. Many practitioners come to know their limitations and preferences as therapists and attempt to select only those clients with whom they ordinarily achieve favorable results.

A second objective of evaluation can best be understood in the context of the social psychology of the professional staff in a clinic or hospital. The treatment of individuals with emotional and behavioral disorders falls far short of being an exact applied science. Yet, despite the uncertainties and ambiguities, decisions affecting the client must be reached and actions initiated. In situations where it is difficult to know what to do, it is helpful to have consensual validation of one's judgment by colleagues. A formal diagnostic evaluation of a client sometimes adds little information but can serve as an "objective" assessment upon which a treatment program can be based.

A third objective of evaluation is often to arrive at a diagnostic classification for purposes of statistical record-keeping.A fourth is to achieve an understanding of the client's problems. The latter two objectives will mainly occupy us in the remainder of the chapter, since these are the official concerns of clinical psychology. Although the second objective—consensual validation—is well known to every candid observer of mental health treatment centers, it is not widely sanctioned.

LIMITATIONS AND ACHIEVEMENTS
OF DIAGNOSIS

The concept of diagnosis, as we have noted, probably originated in general medicine and was then extended to mental health because such problems were, until comparatively recently, almost completely within the purview of the medical profession. In the most general terms, diagnostic evaluation is a process by which a client's problem, as he experiences it, is transformed, through the use of specialized procedures, into a more or less precise statement of his condition in a technical language. Technical communication is characterized by being denotative and by having referents to replicable operations. The language of contemporary medical diagnosis is a mixture of technical and nontechnical statements. To the extent that a diagnosis ultimately rests on validated and reliable examination or laboratory procedures, it is technical; to the extent that it rests upon the patient's reports of his experience, it is not.

One example of the limitations of diagnosis is the patient's report of the location, degree, and type of pain he is suffering. While the experience of pain is very real, it is extremely refractory to quantification. To be sure, it is possible to obtain polygraphic reflections of the subjective experience of pain, but certainly no valid metric has emerged. If medicine aspires to be truly scientific, it must envision some time when every diagnostic statement will rest on replicable procedures producing valid and reliable measurements. Many physicians argue that their profession will always be a craft, and that the art of medicine will always play a significant role in making diagnoses and conducting successful treatment. But, while there is ample support for accepting an artist's understanding as valid, we must take his insight as a given. There is no means to reconstruct his insights, and hence the artist cannot teach anyone else to replicate his creative acts.

If there is much art in the practice of medicine, there is also much science. Countless disease processes and pathological conditions can be accurately and unequivocally detected, and these diagnostic operations can be fully communicated not only to physicians but also to laboratory technicians. These conspicuous achievements have been made because it has been possible to adduce criteria against which diagnostic procedures can be measured. Increasingly sophisticated laboratory and postmorten examination procedures have provided the medical scientist with a powerful tool for sharpening diagnostic techniques. Today it is a rare disease indeed that can escape detection in a properly equipped diagnostic center with appropriately trained personnel. Of course, many more pathological conditions can be identified than can be effectively treated, and there is often a disconcerting discrepancy between the pathology uncovered and the level of well-being and functioning reported by the patient. But it is unassailable that if a pathological condition can be reliably defined, valid diagnostic signs can ordinarily be established.

EVOLUTION OF DIAGNOSTIC PROCEDURES

Diagnosis and treatment in medicine has evolved through several stages, and it may be instructive to look at these schematically. In the earliest phase, one can conjecture that the patient and the diagnostician-therapist were more or less on a par. Both were in full possession of all that the society offered in the way of technology and could, therefore, freely exchange roles, or, if necessary, treat themselves.

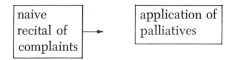

A second stage finds the role of healer differentiated but without the existence of effective remedies by our present standards. To enhance his role, the healer might elaborate a formal language to describe the patient's condition and devise a set of diagnostic categories. He could, likewise, elaborate a set of cures which would be meticulously applied in terms of his system.

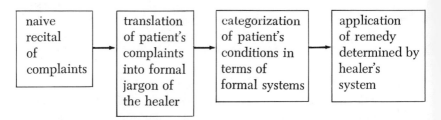

As is readily evident, this paradigm can accommodate the medicine of nonliterate societies, folk medicine, and, indeed, the practices of many contemporary healers who hold rigidly to a one-factor theory of disease. The custom of translating the patient's complaints into Latin, which has persisted into the twentieth century, was no doubt a remnant of this stage. The physician's knowledge of Latin scarcely improved his technical skills, but it helped add a dimension of status and mystery to his performance, thereby enhancing the faith of his patients in his powers. It is noteworthy that the rates of cure of these practitioners were and are often satisfactorily high—often better, in fact, than those of scientific Western medicine for patients with rather diffuse psychological or psychosomatic complaints who have faith in the procedures (Lambo, 1964).

The third stage of evaluation of diagnostic procedures was one in which considerable effort was made to convert formal communications about symptoms into technical statements. Within the limits imposed by the language, physicians attempted to introduce a rough metric into statements about a patient's condition. Thus, close attention to location, smell, color, size, shape, consistency, and so on of manifestations on the surface of the body or palpable beneath the skin, together with a commonly shared and relatively exact knowledge of gross anatomy, enabled physicians to communicate reasonably accurate statements of syndromes and relate these to reports of postmortem examinations or to close descriptions of the course of diseases. Effectiveness of treatment could, in turn, be systematically examined in the light of observed changes in these several parameters.

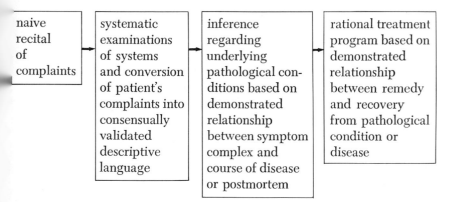

The chart above suggests an invariable relationship between comprehension of a pathological condition, as reflected in a diagnostic statement, and choice of treatment. This relationship is, of course, one always to be sought, but, until comparatively recently, it has been highly qualified. Like many socially important applied sciences, medicine places a high value on results. Consequently, many remedies have been developed on a raw empirical basis—remedies that seem to work, although their actual effect on the pathology underlying the symptoms is not well understood.

For reasons we shall discuss later, psychiatry is among the medical specialities that have been most highly dependent upon simple empiricism. At the same time, because psychiatry is more exposed to public scrutiny and lay involvement than many other specialties, modifications in treatment have often followed from economic and political pressures, or from efforts to conform to humanistic values established by the general community, rather than from adherence to validated, scientific findings.

The final stage in the evolution of medicine might be characterized by the following scheme:

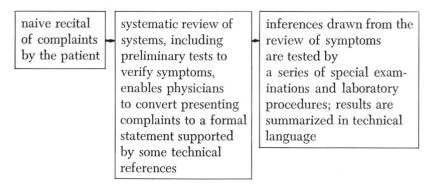

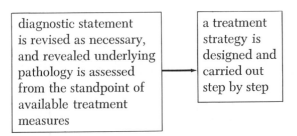

DIAGNOSTIC VOCABULARY AND
THE CRITERIA OF PATHOLOGY

As a branch of medicine, psychiatry necessarily participates in whatever view of pathology is commonly held by the medical profession. Essentially, modern medicine holds that there are many disease entities sufficiently circumscribed to be accurately assessed and distributed into meaningful diagnostic categories. The categories are meaningful because they reflect the "cause" of the observed symptoms and dictate certain treatment measures.

While he is aware that any given disease may have wide ramifications across several systems, the internist finds it most useful to think in terms of identifying and treating primary diseases. That is, the accumulation of clinical knowledge and the development of refined diagnostic devices permit the internists to look beyond an array of observable sysmptoms to an underlying condition that can be designated, for practical purposes, as the cause of the patient's complaints. Once the cause is established, a rational program of treatment can be instituted—a program that takes into account both the underlying condition and the observable manifestations.

As an example of the diagnosis of emotional problems, let us attempt to fit a typical intake procedure to the model given in the last chart above. The first step in the psychodiagnostic assessment is identical to that in any medical specialty: the patient states his complaints in his own language. The second step is also similar to other medical procedures: the interviewer systematically reviews significant areas of the patient's functioning—not primarily bodily function, but his effectiveness in several important areas of living and his level of comfort with his own performance. That is, the interviewer attempts to find out in some detail how severe the symptoms are, when they occur, how often they occur, and how much they affect the patient's work, social life, and recreation, and view of himself. An important part of this second step should also be, minimally, converting the patient's statements into a consensually validated formal language and, ideally, into a technical statement based on reliable measurement. Further, the evaluation should yield tentative hypotheses about the underlying condition, hypotheses that can be established by additional specialized examinations.

It is quite clear that diagnostic studies by psychiatrists and clinical psychologists fall short on all these criteria. There is not one commonly accepted formal vocabulary but many; adherents to any single scheme vary considerably in the inferences they draw from examination data; finally, there is no agreement that the concept of underlying condition is generally viable for psychiatric illness. For a complete review of the issues and related research, see Zigler and Phillips (1961*a* and *b*), who have written a most informative summary and critique of the literature on psychiatric diagnosis.

ACTUARIAL, EMPIRICAL, AND MULTILEVEL APPROACHES

Even if psychodiagnostic assessment were viewed as analogous to a laboratory procedure (a position most clinical psychologists indignantly reject), it is difficult to see just how this function could be carried out. The value of a laboratory procedure is no greater than the validity and reliability of the criteria against which it is measured, and it is far from certain that reliable criteria can be adduced in respect to most emotional and behavioral problems (other than for some that have been established as having unambiguous organic etiology). Considerations such as these have led many psychiatrists and clinical psychologists to suggest that psychiatric disorders should not be considered in the same frame of reference as illnesses that are the concern of internal medicine. While biologically based medicine can be reductionistic in principle (that is, manifest symptoms can eventually be correlated with anatomical findings and understood in terms of biophysics and biochemistry), emotional and behavioral symptoms, they maintain, cannot. The proper study for psychiatrists and clinical psychologists, they claim, is the *psychology* of man, and psychological statements should not be translated into the language of neurophysiology or neuroanatomy.

Parenthetically, it should be added that an interest group comprised of mental health administrators and biostatisticians must also be entered in the record, for psychologists have been invited to assist them in solving their particular problems with the assessment of psychiatric conditions.

These officials are responsible for deriving an accurate picture of the mental health of a community in order to recommend a rational program of care for the present and to formulate realistic plans for the future. They are, therefore, not necessarily identified with either the biological or psychological wings of psychiatry but are eager to have from any source some reliable device for assigning patients to meaningful categories. In their terms, a meaningful categorization says something about the degree of a patient's social impairment, the course and length of his illness, and his probable requirements in terms of rehabilitation. No existing classification scheme adequately meets these needs.

Returning to those who reject a medical model, let us examine the premises on which they develop their approach to clinical assessment. Clearly, their most fundamental and inescapable assumption is that psychic events have primacy. The implication is that whatever internal or external stimulation may be stirring the human organism at the biological or interpersonal levels, the significant events for the psychiatrist and clinical psychologist are psychological. Their interest is in how the individual human at the psychological level assimilates and structures data impinging upon him and how, in turn, he conceptualizes his response. Clinical assessment in these terms then becomes a matter of tuning in accurately on how a patient construes himself and the psychologically relevant parameters, both past and present, of the world around him.

For assistance in their work, clinicians who are psychologically oriented draw upon mentalistic theories of personality that hypothesize certain regularities in the relationships between psychic events and between psychic events and clinically relevant behavior. Space does not permit a review of competing theories, although some will be briefly covered in Chapters 4–7 in connection with theories of psychotherapy. The reader can refer to Hall and Lindzey (1957), Wepman and Heine (1963), or Maddi (1968) for succinct but authoritative summaries of the most widely known personality theories. One parameter along which these theories differ is the extent to which unconscious mental events figure and are deemed motivational. For several decades, the psychoanalytic theory of Sigmund Freud or derivatives from it have dominated American psychiatry, and the concept of an unconscious psychic system interacting with a conscious system is a central article of faith. Since most clinical psychologists have been reared in this theoretical atmosphere, they find one or another of the psychoanalytic theories compatible to their needs. However, recourse to a multilevel model of mental events is not essential to a psychological approach to clinical assessment. For example, in the early 1950s, G. A. Kelly (1955) devised a scheme for comprehending human behavior in terms of the individual's "personal construct system," a system derivable by using a prescribed technique in questioning the subject.

It is apparent that treating emotional and behavioral disorders from a purely psychological standpoint enormously increases the scope of the clinical psychologist's field of action. On the one hand, he no longer has to wait until the biological sciences offer data against which to test diagnostic devices. On the other, he is not obliged to participate in the tedious, time-consuming, and somewhat unrewarding task of trying to devise internally consistent, reliably differentiated, and accurately predictive diagnostic categories.

Within the framework of a psychiatry that holds its proper study to be the type and interrelationship of psychological events in the patient, the aim of clinical assessment is understanding, comprehension, or insight. This statement implies an objective not ordinarily associated with science. But what is generally meant by understanding is an idiographic account of how a wide variety of observations (some of which may seem to be contradictory) can be integrated into one coherent depiction of an individual's personality functioning. Diagnostic categories, by contrast, are nomothetic in that they depict a particular class of psychopathological disorders by constellations of observable symptoms that tend to occur together. Conventional psychiatric diagnosis involves matching a patient's present symptoms to those defining one or another of the categories in a classification scheme; a patient is then said to have the disorder that corresponds most closely with his symptoms. Clearly, this is a somewhat circular process. While a practitioner may be induced to examine a patient more systematically if he is guided by a classificatory scheme, there are few inferences he can draw from the diagnosis, once it is made, that he could not draw from the symptoms themselves.

In a psychoanalytic evaluation of a patient, the practitioner does not match symptoms to empirically derived categories, but instead places his observations within the context of a theory that provides a coherent framework and serves as a heuristic device. The clinical psychologist following this approach considers his work complete when he has accounted for all the sampled behavior of the patient in a way that is consonant with his theoretical point of view. An internally consistent statement that incorporates all or most of the observational data and extrapolates from these data by judicious use of theory constitutes understanding.

More specifically, a typical formulation postulates one or more conflicts, impulses, wishes, or fixations which, although outside the patient's awareness, are seeking overt expression in behavior that is either socially unacceptable or contrary to the patient's moral standards. The formulation then describes the defenses the patient is employing to forestall the eruption of unacceptable behavior and the conditions under which he is working. Symptoms are viewed merely as maladaptive, defensive efforts. Efforts to avoid the anxiety generated when an unacceptable, unconscious motive threatens to emerge are what stimulates the formation of defenses. Roughly speaking, the intensity of the anxiety experienced is correlated with the degree of pathology observed.

It might seem both desirable and necessary for the analytically oriented practitioner to devise a classification scheme based on his own concepts and methods of data collection. That is, by observing systematically the association of certain patterns of defense and symptom formation with certain constellations of anxiety-generating unconscious impulses, it might be possible to identify recurring types. While such a scheme might have many of the shortcomings of other diagnostic classifications, it would have the advantage of consolidating a specialized vocabulary, sharpening etiological concepts, and focusing communication around treatment issues and prognosis.

Such efforts have been undertaken, particularly with respect to psychosomatic symptoms (Alexander 1950; Dunbar 1954), but have floundered on the stubborn functional equivalence and equifinality of disparate patterns of psychic events. Patterns of conflict and defense judged to be quite different from one another often produce similar observable symptoms, while studies of individuals with phenotypically similar reaction patterns disclose widely different underlying psychic structures.

In the end, psychologically oriented practitioners have had to accept empirically derived patterns of observable symptoms as the most workable basis of classification of emotional and behavioral disorders. They have, however, had an important influence on how contemporary diagnostic schemes are viewed. Instead of regarding particular syndromes as diseases in the classical biological sense of the term, diagnostic categories are now treated merely as patterns of reaction which, while sometimes highly stable and refractory to modification, are simply the surface manifestations of a continually changing, dynamic psychic system. Philosophically, such a modification is extremely important, since it abandons the pessimistic position that mental illnesses are immutable and substitutes the relatively optimistic view that undesirable reactions can be altered with appropriate intervention, or even spontaneously.

Robbins (1966), together with his one-time colleagues Robert Wallerstein and Karl Menninger, has devoted much effort to examining systematically the problems of assessment and prediction within a psychoanalytic model of personality. His conclusions are succinctly stated in the following quotation: (pp. 25–26)

1. Mental illness derives from otherwise insoluble conflicts.
2. These conflicts are in large part unconscious.
3. Intrapsychic conflicts are related to early childhood experiences and represent inadequately resolved infantile conflicts.
4. Prior to the onset of clinical illness, the intrapsychic conflicts are handled through the idiosyncratic patterning of impulse-defense configurations, character traits, and perhaps more or less ego-syntonic symptoms, which together make up the personality structure of the individual.
5. Through varying combinations of inner and outer stresses (sometimes clearly discernible as "precipitating events"), the previously utilized methods of maintaining homeostatic equilibrium fail, and symptoms or ego-dystonic character traits, or both, appear.
6. The patterning of the symptoms and associated ego-dystonic character traits reveals important elements of the inner conflicts, the ways the ego tries to cope with them, as well as important aspects of the fundamental character organization of the individual.

This definition contains etiological concepts, relates mental illnesses to normal personality, and views them as disturbances in psychological processes common to all but combined uniquely for an individual. It makes no effort to classify or order mental illnesses even though it appears to offer a basis for considering their etiology. Although it too focuses on intrapsychic processes, considers the relationship between the phenomena of the illness and the personality of the person who is ill, and includes the impact of past life experiences and current stresses as significant factors, it still leaves important questions unanswered. One basic question is whether the intrapsychic conflicts are causative or pathoplastic. While we can safely say that *much* of the behavior of mentally ill patients can be understood as stemming from insoluble conflicts, we cannot state that this is true of *all* of their pathological behavior.

Furthermore, it must be acknowledged that although we can, utilizing psychonanalytic concepts, reach a fairly reasonable understanding of much that is occurring psychologically in people and account for much of their behavior (whether it be viewed as healthy or unhealthy), we are not yet able to predict accurately whether a given person, with a particular history, will become ill under given stresses, nor can we predict precisely what form his illness will take.

In summary, then, psychologists play a major role in three assessment tasks. Each of these, however, has had a somewhat independent development, and there is surprisingly little overlap in the techniques em-

ployed. Those psychologists who have preferred to work in terms of the
conventional, medical-biological model have sought to make relatively
precise measurements of psychological functions and performance capacities demonstratably altered by impairment of the brain. Psychologists
concerned with institutional administration, including the economical
classification and evaluation of large populations of patients, have used
sophisticated statistical techniques to develop inventories, scales, and
rating devices on a relatively pure empirical basis. However, the majority
of psychologists in clinical settings have become deeply involved in using
a variety of free-response procedures as a medium for arriving at an
understanding of the dynamics of individual patients. This last group
takes its inspiration from statements like that of Robbins quoted
above.

Each of these three major groups in clinical psychology has defined
the problem of assessment differently, and each has attempted to answer
differently the questions it has set for itself. Although their assessment
tasks are logically distinct enterprises, psychologists identified with each
of the three approaches have engaged in a good bit of sniping at one
another. Debates have most often occurred between proponents of
actuarial versus clinical methods of assessment and have, to some
measure, derived from a failure on the part of the antagonist to recognize
that they often perform dissimilar tasks.

To be sure, there has been a certain amount of trading off of techniques, or at least borrowing of test materials, which are then reworked
into the theoretical framework of the borrower. Thus, for example, the
Rorschach Ink Blots—which are widely used by and closely identified
with the psychodynamic, individual approach to assessment—have been
administered to groups (Munroe 1941; Harrower-Erickson 1941, 1943);
and a new and greatly expanded (43 vs. 10) set of blots (Holtzman et al.
1960) was designed from the beginning to be open to analysis of psychometric properties. Carson (1968) has proposed a technique for analyzing
a patient's Minnesota Multiphasic Personality Inventory profile in psychodynamic terms, while virtually every well-trained journeyman clinician
can interpret a patient's responses to the Wechsler Adult Intelligence
Scale in psychodynamic terms, even though the instrument was designed
and is most generally employed as a psychometric device.

ASSESSMENT TASKS AND THE
UTILITY OF TECHNIQUES

To understand the current use of psychological assessment devices, the
variety of assessment tasks confronting psychologists must be clearly

lelineated. As one example, let us consider a psychologist in an admissions office of a university. The director of admissions poses the following problem: The university can accept only 1 of every 3 among 6000 eligible applicants. It is therefore important to select those students who can make the best use of the opportunity. Moreover, the admissions office can afford only one psychologist to assist in making the selection. The psychologist realizes immediately that he cannot personally evaluate 6000 applicants and must, therefore, proceed along actuarial lines. That is, he will use assessment devices that do not involve judgments about individual students but that will increase the probability of admitting students of the calibre sought and correspondingly reduce the probability of admitting students who will fail.

Before the psychologist begins his work, he must resolve the question, "What do you mean by 'make the best use of the opportunity'?" Such a statement could refer to any number of personally and socially relevant values and aspirations of the applicants. It could refer to vocational achievements after graduation, or to independent measures of achievement in the students' areas of concentration. All except the last, however, are probably too difficult to measure reliably.

Consequently, the director of admissions will be constrained to acknowledge that he will be content if the selection devices estimate the probability of an applicant's passing his courses and successfully completing his bachelor's degree. Given this criterion, the psychologist can confidently select instruments that have been demonstrated to predict successful performance in college level course work. Over time, he can further refine such selection procedures for use in the particular university setting with the particular population of applicants for which he is responsible.

It should be noted that scholastic aptitude tests (which are essentially tests of intellectual performance on a sample of verbal and quantitative problems) are far from perfect, since they cannot take into account either personality factors (such as motivation, work habits, and character) or the social experiences of the students after they are admitted. Indeed, the correlations between test scores and grades are at a level that would make prediction about any single student extremely hazardous. Nevertheless, on an actuarial basis they are very useful in reducing the proportion of students who are admitted and subsequently fail.

Why are personality factors not weighed in selection for admission? Most simply stated, the psychological tests that purport to measure such factors and can be given to groups and economically scored do not add enough to the predictive efficiency of selection procedures based on grades and scholastic aptitude tests to justify the time or expense of administering them. Decisions made on the basis of such tests would also be more difficult to defend to parents or legislators than those based or intellectual performance.

Suppose, however, that the parents of a high school student are interested in determining whether or not he would succeed in college. A counselor faced with such a question would have recourse to standard measures of aptitude for college level work and to measures of academic achievement, but, to provide a responsible answer, he would also have to develop a great deal more information about the student. Through interviews, the counselor would attempt to ascertain the objectives of college attendance for the student—and the balance of prospective gratifications and disappointments. He would try to discern the student's characteristic pattern of handling stress, his habits of work, his social maturity, his degree of involvement in intellectual interests as contrasted with practical pursuits, and so on.

He might then supplement his interviews with projective tests from which he could deduce feelings, attitudes, fears, and patterns of problem-solving largely outside the student's awareness but, nevertheless, deemed motivational, either generally or in certain situations. He would, no doubt, pursue all these lines of inquiry in order to give a responsible answer to the questions posed by the student and his parents, but the thoroughness of his inquiry would be no guarantee of the accuracy of his prediction.

There are no data to support the belief that a clinician using such familiar techniques can better predict firm performance criteria such as grade point averages in college or the likelihood of passing in a training situation than actuarially based instruments. Indeed, the predictive record of experienced clinicians has been uniformly disappointing (Kelly and Fiske 1951; Holtzman and Sells 1954; Holt and Luborsky 1958). In many other situations involving diffuse or unstable criteria that cannot be reliably measured, no one can be expected to do well, for the validity coefficient of an assessment technique cannot ordinarily rise above the reliability of the criteria measure. It should also be noted that occasionally a naive clinician with greater faith in his skills than good sense is trapped into making predictions without knowing the base rate for occurrence of the events being predicted. If, for example, he knew that only one in a hundred patients discharged from his hospital with a diagnosis of schizophrenia would not apply for further treatment, he would be wise to predict in any given case that further treatment would be required, regardless of his test results.

How can a psychodynamically oriented clinician be of use when he is asked to make a judgment regarding an individual? If, as is frequently the case, a categorical judgment is sought ("Should Johnny be sent to special school or can he make it in a regular class?" "Does Mrs. Jones require hospitalization or can she be treated on an outpatient basis?" "What is the probability that Mr. Brown will commit suicide if he is released from the hospital?" "Can Mr. Black get along with his family if we give him a weekend pass?"), he may have to offer an opinion, but he would be unwise to place too much credence in his own pronouncements. What the able clinician should be able to do (and apparently is able to do often enough to command a loyal company of consumers) is to develop hypotheses about conflicts, ambivalences, anxieties and uncertainties, fears and defenses that seem to accurately characterize an individual's view of himself and his situation.

The clinician deals almost exclusively with balances and resultants of forces—with an individual's potential for responding in particular ways to particular situations. His goal is understanding or insight rather than accuracy of prediction of specific responses to specific life circumstances. The clinician would say with some justification that he cannot predict specific behaviors because he neither knows nor can he control the array of social environmental forces impinging upon a subject at any given time, and he cannot explore the particular meaning of every significant event in an individual's life in advance of the event.

Clearly, what the clinical approach to assessment can do that other techniques cannot do is stimulate a broader and deeper examination of a subject's life situation. It may be true that a clinical evaluation cannot greatly improve upon a scholastic aptitude test battery in predicting grade point average. But it does draw attention to many aspects of intellectual functioning—apprehensions, conflicts, inhibitions, and potentialities—that might otherwise be ignored. For example, a clinician may see indications that many problems of the client are dramatized in terms of a dependency-independency conflict. Any honest clinician will acknowledge that he cannot, on the basis of this observation, predict the behavior of a client in a given situation. At the same time, the observation does provide a framework for the client to examine in some depth his reactions to significant people and situations. Thus, the experience of the clinical assessment itself may offer beneficial insights to the client, or alert him to personal propensities over which he can exert conscious control in his own interests. Further, the clinical assessment may reveal problems for which remedial steps can be taken. Not all of these outcomes follow from every clinical assessment, but obviously none of them can occur when an individual takes tests in an impersonal group situation.

Nevertheless, there is no way of measuring understanding. Only the consequences of understanding can be measured, and by consequences one ordinarily refers to events that can be reliably witnessed. To be sure, the attribution of validity to a clinician's insight might be increased if ten clinicians looking at the same data all came up with the same result. Unfortunately, clinicians have gained very little more comfort from efforts at consensual validation of their interpretations of clinical data than from their efforts to predict outcomes (Datel and Gengerelli 1955; Little and Shneidman 1955).

It may be some small comfort for the clinician to realize that he has for company seismologists, volcanologists, meteorologists, ethologists, ecologists, economists, and other specialists who work with complex inter-action of forces that cannot be experimentally controlled. Although these natural and social scientists undoubtedly have a better record for con-sensual validation of their interpretation of data, the predictive validity of their statements is in most instances not correspondingly high. Some of them do have the benefit of well-developed criteria of the accuracy of their predictions, which psychologists frequently lack.

THE DEVELOPMENT OF INSTRUMENTS AND METHODS

These few remarks on the peculiar problems of psychodynamically ori-ented clinical psychology do no more than introduce the subject. It may be of value to examine one or two of the instruments and methods used in clinical assessment in order to understand the terms on which a rapprochement with scientific psychology might be achieved.

Psychological assessment had its origins in a scientific concern over individual differences which, in turn, had its roots in the revolutions of the eighteenth and nineteenth centuries. The probable reason for this concern is not difficult to infer. Individual differences in personality, like other differences, are differences only when they make a difference. In societies in which the individual is fixed by his membership in a social category from which he cannot escape, personal attributes are not unnoticed, but they are simply not very important. But the revolts of the burgeois against the royal autocrats and the later so-called prole-tarian revolutions created meritocracies in which there was open compe-tition for education and the associated status and opportunity. Only in a society which is to some degree open, where upward and horizontal mobility are possible and even encouraged, do individual differences be-come highly significant. If everyone in class X is provided with an edu-cation and everyone in class Y is not, it does not matter what degree of educability is possessed by an individual in class X or in class Y. If, on the other hand, everyone is educated up to the limits of his capacity, ɔut there are facilities available at advanced levels only for some fraction ɔf the whole, then it is imperative to develop a procedure for determining individual differences in capacity. If some facilities are available for everyone, it is then imperative to determine for what type and level of training an individual is fitted.

It would not be unreasonable to attribute the greatly increased interest in psychotherapy and personal counseling to the same source. As a society becomes more supportive of upward or horizontal mobility, each individual feels more keenly the onus of his own failure to achieve or to find the right niche, and he may therefore seek to remove any personal impediment through intensive self-evaluation and self-investigation with professional assistance.

In any event, the scientific interest in individual differences is a nineteenth- and twentieth-century phenomenon. One early stimulus may have been furnished in 1796 by Maskelyne, the Astronomer Royal at Greenwich, when he fired Kinnebrook, his assistant, for differing with him by eight-tenths of a second in timing the transit of a star across the hairline of a telescope. Maskelyne viewed this difference as stemming from incompetence, whereas Bessel, the astronomer at Köningsberg, after testing various observers under similar conditions, concluded that the so-called errors of observers were irreducible differences due to the "personal equation." Unfortunately, Bessel could not save Kinnebrook's job, since he did not get around to his crude but significant experiments until 1819.

In 1884, Sir Francis Galton established a laboratory in England in which he developed tests of sensory acuity, motor skills, and intellectual and physical abilities. With Pearson, he also developed the statistical methods necessary to deal with his results, including the concept of correlation (the degree of covariation of two measures). There were parallel developments of simple tests for sensory, motor, and perceptual skills in America, using quantitative methods, by James McKean Cattell and Joseph Jastrow.

As early as 1890, Binet in France began changing the trend by shifting attention from simple sensory and motor abilities to complex, higher mental processes. Binet first published a scale in 1905 in which he established that, by administering to children groups of tests graded in difficulty, he could establish norms of intellectual ability for different age groups. This, of course, meant that he could identify the more and less educable children. There were revisions in 1908 and in 1911, the year in which the scale was first translated into English. In 1916, Terman published the Stanford revision of the Binet scale, and a new revision was published in 1937 (Terman 1916; Terman and Merrill 1937). Meanwhile, a variety of tests categorized as achievement, aptitude, intelligence, and personality tests were developed (1300 tests were developed between 1917 and 1928, and by 1940, 2600). These were both individual and group tests.

The successive revisions of the measures of intelligence were based on data accumulated through their actual use in practical situations and had several objectives. Among these were better standardization through improved procedures of administration and revision of content. Most important, however, for those tests which were widely used for diagnostic purposes was better normative data based on improved sampling of the population for which the test was designed.

No matter how ingenious a psychologist may be in his development of a test, its value as a diagnostic instrument depends on how closely the sample of clients on which the instrument was originally tested corresponds to the client population on which it is to be used.

If a test is designed to be used nationally (to say nothing of internationally) the population on which the test is originally developed should be a faithful replication of the entire population of the country.

Clearly in a country such as ours—with regional, racial, national, economic, urban, rural, vocational, and educational fctors to be considered—this is an objective difficult if not impossible to achieve. For example, in this country, whites, on the average, obtain somewhat higher scores on standard intelligence tests than do blacks. Experts now believe that this is because most American blacks have not had social and educational experiences comparable to the population on which the tests were standardized. One hardly need add that not all tests are standardized on national stratified samples, but on more restricted samples drawn from the populations with which they will be used. The Wechsler-Bellevue and Wechsler Adult Intelligence Scale—(Wechsler 1955, 1958) the most widely used adult scales—are, likewise, standardized with considerable regard for sampling of the general population for whom the battery is designed. There are some relatively serious omissions in the samplings, but these are too technical and detailed to detain us here.

In summary, then, from early beginnings in measuring individual differences in sensory acuity, psychologists have developed techniques for reliably measuring complex mental functions through the use of groups of separate tests, individually standardized and then brought together and standardized and scaled as a single battery. These tests provide a sound basis for examining mental functioning both qualitatively and, through the development of appropriate statistical devices, quantitatively. Qualitatively, it is possible to describe those intellectual functions in which an individual is relatively rich and relatively poor. Quantitatively, it is possible to compare an individual's composite score with that of another person and describe their relative standing in the general population.

A method of psychological investigation deriving from a quite different tradition than the psychometric approach are the so-called projective techniques, which are characterized by more or less free responses to more or less unstructured stimuli. In the psychometric approach, there is a one specific correct answer, or at best a limited number of alternatives, for each specific question. Projective techniques provide for a much wider scope of response. The subject is asked to draw a figure, tell a story, or interpret an inkblot without full awareness that a number of variables in his response will be analyzed and interpreted and conclusions drawn regarding his personality characteristics.

The history of the use of such stimuli is as old as the psychometric tradition. Galton, in 1879, experimented with free association. Cattell and Bryant, in 1889, also studied free association. Binet studied responses to inkblots in 1895. G. Stanley Hall studied daydreams and stories written in response to pictures in 1907 (antedating Henry Murray and the Thematic Apperception Test by almost thirty years). However, these early investigators were interested only in classifying responses and using them in estimating the mental development of a person, rather than as an avenue to the understanding of a subject's inner life.

Until projective tests came into general use, virtually all exploration of human behavior by tests was predicated on the existence of a normative group. The performance of the individual had no meaning except in relationship to the average performance and the range of performance of a well-defined sample of people. The interpretation of an individual's performance, even on personality inventories, was always stated in these terms, and the entire operation was strictly empirical.

To say that the development and interpretation of tests was empirical says nothing about their quality or utility. Many tests are very poorly conceived, poorly developed, poorly interpreted, and altogether lacking in utility. They are, however, open to criticism on essentially empirical grounds and subject to refinement by well-developed techniques. Behavior on tests (the pattern of response to the items comprising the test) is correlated with criterion behavior. The utility of a test is judged by the extent to which behavior on the test predicts criterion behavior. Until relatively recently, no assumptions were made about the processing of the experience by the test-taker. That is, the test-taker's attitude and motivations with respect to the testing situation were not taken into consideration in test development. Current researchers are, however, very alert to test-taking strategies and have developed some scoring devices for taking these factors into account.

The contributions to clinical assessments from this early period were considerable, but they were primarily in the area of measuring and evaluating intellectual functioning. The testing procedures were no more than highly systematic evaluations of performance on several intellectual and judgmental tasks. Because these tests were both comprehensive (as the term "comprehensive" was understood at that time) and standardized, more reliable information could be obtained from them, on the average, than from a clinical appraisal using interviews or such devises as are available in physicians' guides for doing a mental status examination.

Several other clinical assessment procedures using the psychometric method were devised during the same period; I shall mention only one as an example. The Elgin Prognostic Scale (Wittman 1941) involved systematic study of patient characteristics against the criterion of length of stay in a mental hospital. Since the scale took systematic account of almost *every* patient characteristic associated with length of stay, it could, on the average, predict a patient's career better than clinicians could from their interviews.

In making assessments of a patient, a clinician uses the same kinds of data as a test, scale, or inventory. However, he generally does not use *all* the relevant data; he does not use the information he gains systematically; and he does not know (except intuitively) how to weigh the relative importance of the data he does obtain. Thus, if there is a reliable and valid criterion against which to measure the utility of information, a test is always a better predictor, on the average, than is a clinician (Meehl 1954).

MODERN PROJECTIVE TESTS

With the advent of Freudian psychoanalytic theory, both psychiatry and psychology were faced with a rather complicated issue. Observable behavior (verbal and physical) was now to be viewed as but the surface reflection of events that, by their very nature, could not be observed. Symptoms were to be viewed as only one aspect of a dynamic system, the most potent forces in which were obscured by the patient's defenses. The patient's verbalizations were to be regarded not as revealing of significant information but as unwitting attempts to deceive—to keep hidden the unacceptable feelings, impulses, wishes, and conflicts that were the real motivations.

There have been two major lines of attack on this problem: (1) reading between the lines as it were—not taking at face value what the patient reports or how he behaves but being alert for contradictions, omissions, inconsistencies, forgetfulness, peculiar emphases, and the like which would provide a key to what was behind the facade; and (2) circumventing the defenses by deceit—asking the patient to respond to seemingly innocuous stimuli or to perform innocuous tasks which are sufficiently ambiguous to quiet any anxiety he may have that his defenses are being breached.

The second approach refers, of course, to the "projective" tests—a term first used by Lawrence Frank (1939). Quotation marks have been added to the word because, while the subject may indeed construct (as in the Rorschach Ink Blots) objects out of neutral or ambiguous stimuli, objects to which he attributes thoughts, feelings, and attitudes, he does many other things as well. Given the general criterion of being a task or a stimulus that places no formal restraints on the patient's involvement, the media through which projection can be induced are practically limitless. Because stimuli are essentially neutral, the response is what is important. Drawings, paintings, sculpture, arrangement of figures and objects, free play—in fact, virtually any unstructured stimuli are suitable and have been employed.

Frank (1948) has classified these devices into five categories: (1) constitutive—for example, clay modeling, drawing; (2) constructive—organizing toy figures; (3) interpretive—interpreting pictures, cloud pictures, or inkblots; (4) cathartic—forceful handling of materials or doll figures; and (5) expressive—gestures, posture, handwriting, voice, speech, gait, and so on. This variety of devices can pull from the patient more or less unguarded expressions of himself, some of which can be interpreted as reflecting thoughts, feelings, attitudes, and impulses of which he is either unaware or that he is ordinarily unwilling to disclose. Moreover, innumerable variables in these responses can be assessed qualitatively or quantitatively with considerable reliability. Finally, the responses involve the whole person in that he is consciously utilizing his intelligence, is affectively aroused, and reveals his characteristic problem-solving style in coming to grips with the task. Moreover, he is providing information about himself which he ordinarily views as private or which he cannot voluntarily offer since it is outside of conscious awareness.

It must have seemed to such innovators as David Levy (1937), Hermann Rorschach (1942), and, later, Henry Murray (1938) that they were truly ushering in a new era in which the tools were now available to disclose fully the inner workings of human personality. At the inception of their use, it is likely that many psychologists believed free response techniques to be as important in relation to psychological assessment as the microscope had been to medical diagnosis. It must have seemed that it was only a matter of perfecting techniques of administration, analysis, and interpretation before highly accurate depictions of the dynamics of personality could be routinely turned out by adequately trained individuals. The enthusiasm with which clinical psychologists embraced projective devices has not, however, proved to be altogether warranted. These tools continue to be widely used and strongly defended, but a great deal of painstaking research needs to be done even to delineate their potentialities as assessment devices.

Many clinical psychologists have, in fact, rejected the view that projective devices are tests that can be evaluated with the same methods that are applied to psychometric instruments. The free response procedures, they argue, should be thought of as interview aids, and the proper object of research should be the psychologist and his use of the instrument rather than the test itself. Space will not permit detailed examination of all projective devices in common use, but a description of two such widely used procedures—the Rorschach Ink Blots and the Thematic Apperception Test—may help illustrate some of the interpretive problems associated with them.

The Rorschach Test

The Rorschach test is comprised of ten inkblots printed on cards, five of which (numbers I, IV, V, VI, VII) are black on a white background (with various shadings in gray), two of which (II and III) have red areas in addition to the black, and three of which (VIII, IX and X) are multicolored. Since they were originally produced by placing ink on a creased sheet of paper and pressing the halves of the sheet together, the blots are essentially symmetrical forms with a well-defined center line. While the ten blots comprising the set were selected from a much larger number to achieve a range and variety of stimuli, they were not designed to resemble actual objects and are truly accidental productions without intrinsic meaning. Hence, they are subject to innumerable interpretations.

In a conventional administration, the subject is given the cards one at a time in a prescribed order and orientation. Prior to being given the first card, the subject is told simply to report what he sees or what the blots look like to him. If he gives only one response to the first card, he is informed that some respondents give more than one. If he asks questions about procedure or the cards or his responses, he is ordinarily given a noncommital reply which in essence reflects that the testee can do as he pleases. Procedures of administration are by no means standardized, but in general the subject is allowed to interpret and carry out the task in his own way.

What the testee chooses to do varies enormously from one subject to another. An outpatient in a psychiatric clinic once gave the writer nearly 800 responses to the ten blots, and another gave almost 90 responses to one card! More typically, subjects of normal intelligence offer from 20 to 50 distinct responses to the entire series of 10 blots.

Analysis of the subject's responses is carried out in terms of a number of categories for which there are elaborate notational systems. The examiner routinely seeks the answers to the following questions: (1) How did the subject behave toward the examiner and the testing materials? (2) Where in the blot did the subject see the objects reported and how much of the blot was used? (3) What features of the blot contributed to the response? (4) What was the content of the responses reported? (5) How accurate were the perceptions reported? In the vocabulary of Rorschach users, these categories are test behavior, location, determinants, content, and form level. This information is obtained in a detailed way with relevant associations in an inquiry that follows the administration of all ten blots.

Two types of analysis are possible. Both are generally taught to students of clinical psychology, and interpretations are often a blend of the two approaches. The first is based on the notion that a person conducts himself in life as he does on the test and that the psychology of a functioning person is essentially one of checks, balances, and compromises. The testee can maintain a certain distance from the stimulus material. That is, he can say that the inkblot "looks like a bird or a person's face or a flower," but he is sufficiently detached that he does not become upset at his own responses or begin to regard objects seen in the blots as real. For example, seeing a bright red area as a "colorful necktie" or a "Chinese poppy" reflects a capacity to respond to a vivid stimulus with a degree of control that permits enjoyment. A response of "blood" or "a pool of blood" suggests an immediacy of reaction that contains an element of unpleasant shock. The response, "that is my blood" reflects a loss of distance from the stimulus, which in turn suggests a precarious hold on reality.

In using the stimulus material, the testee should be able to see the big picture in the whole blot but also be attentive to some large details and a few small details. The area of the blot in which he reports seeing an object should resemble that object, but he should be willing to ignore a few nonessential discrepancies in form in order to report his discovery. He should make several responses that are common to the majority who have taken the test but not so many that his associations are deemed banal. He should make some unusual or original responses reflecting his unique perceptions of his world but not so many that his fantasy is judged to be bizarre or eccentric. In virtually every dimension of response, the subject is expected either to be balanced in his behavior or to compensate with an outstanding strength for any evident weakness. Deviant performance that remains uncompensated is presumed to indicate a potential personality weakness, while demonstrated strengths are construed as probable assets.

As evident, the examiner's inferences are based on analogy. What the subject does in meeting the demands of the Rorschach test he is also presumed to do in handling the demands he faces in everyday life. The interpeter's task, among others, is to exercise shrewd judgment in determining what constructions of the inkblot have their analogue in the life of a given testee.

The second interpretive approach regards the subject's responses as a reflection of his status and functioning in terms of psychosexual development. The interpreter looks for indications of fixation at or regression to a pregenital level and then attempts to describe the pattern of defenses erected against the emergence of these disorganizing impulses into consciousness and the sphere of behavior. Consonant with the premises of psychoanalytic theory, the subject's efforts to keep troublesome impulses and unconscious conflicts out of awareness are seen as shaping, inhibiting, or distorting all categories of response to the inkblots. The task of the interpreter is to trace the vicissitudes of the instinctual drives as they seek expression in the framework of the subject's personality and to explain responses to the blots in terms of this conflict-defense paradigm.

Thus, any statements about the subject's approach to the problems of living are based on deduction rather than analogy. The interpreter may note, for example, that the subject seems to respond much more frequently to peripheral details of certain blots than to central elements. In the terms of the first approach to interpretation, the subject might be said to have a stable trait of approaching problems circumspectly and getting caught up in nonessential details. The second approach would assume that the circumstantiality was a defense against some anxiety-provoking feature in certain of the blots and that, while circumstantiality might be commonly seen in the subject's behavior, it would more likely occur only in situations where a particular anxiety-provoking impulse was evoked.

There is a measure of empirical support for both of these modes of interpretation, but none so compelling that a psychologist is entitled to rely confidently on any single approach (Zubin 1954).* As noted earlier, interpreters differ widely in their ingenuity, sensitivity, and verbal fluency. And, as in any art, the master is far more perceptive of possible inferences to be drawn from a display of data than is the neophyte. Moreover, in a task as complex and controversial as that of personality diagnosis, there is no effective way of validating insights.

The Criterion Problem

Systematic research in which the subject's responses are reliably defined and then related to a criterion which is also reasonably well defined fails to yield satisfying results. The chief difficulty in pursuing research on clinical assessment lies in the criterion problem. Ordinarily, in pursuing any research involving prediction from one set of events to another, the second set can be accurately and reliably measured. In meteorology, as an example, it is possible to determine rather exactly the amount of precipitation, hours of sunlight, or percent of cloud cover in a given area. What is difficult to find is a discriminate equation giving the proper weight to each of a complicated set of antecedent conditions in order to make an accurate prediction.

Psychologists, on the other hand, have not agreed on accurate and reliable criterion measures. The methods available for evaluating criterion behavior are essentially no different and no more reliable than those measures on the basis of which predictions are made. It is extremely difficult to gain substantial agreement on the extent to which an individual exhibits, let us say, an Oedipal conflict.

The Manipulation Problem

Another fundamental problem being given increasing attention is the degree to which a subject is really deceived by testing procedures designed to circumvent his defenses. There are strong indications that responses can be and are manipulated, especially by perceptive individuals, depending upon the situation in which a test is administered. There are also indications that the set of responses a subject actually gives is only one of several sets he is capable of giving, if he so chooses. This

* The July, 1968, issue of *Psychological Bulletin* (Vol. 70, No. 1) gives a thoroughgoing analysis of the empirical support for the clinical interpretation of one widely used projective device, the Draw-a-Person test. Particularly noteworthy is the high degree of plausibility of the interpretive scheme, juxtaposed to the low level of empirical support.

means that, rather than being the *only* behavior of which the subject is capable, the responses given represent merely one sample of behavior designed to conform to the subject's interpretation of the examiner's intentions and to his estimate of the probable consequences of responding one way rather than another. It is, moreover, quite possible that changes in a subject's response depending upon the circumstances of testing are not fully conscious, deliberate tactical maneuvers. Most individuals have sets of security operations of varying degrees of complexity which are brought into play in response to certain social environmental demands. The subject's approach to the stimulus may reflect a general style of behavior designed either to minimize potential threat or maximize presentation of a particular image of self. This is, of course, very useful information, provided one has some notion of what the subject is trying to achieve, but it is a different type of information from that postulated to flow from the subject's engagement with neutral stimulus material. A prime value of projective tests has rested on the assumption that the subject's responses were more genuine, because unguarded, than responses to printed questionnaires, in which desirable answers are often transparently obvious. Projective devices, in short, are no royal road to the unconscious, nor do they necessarily induce a subject to reveal aspects of self in a totally unguarded manner.

The Thematic Apperception Test

These same general considerations with respect to reliability and validity also apply to the Thematic Apperception Test (TAT), originally devised by Henry Murray (Morgan and Murray 1935) and his associates as a tool in a program of study of careers of students at Harvard University. Murray was particularly impressed with the possibility than an individual's behavior could be understood in terms of a hierarchy of thematic lines that interact with various kinds of social environmental demands. The unfolding of an individual's life over time was the criterion against which Murray and his students hoped to sharpen their conceptual scheme and the assessment procedures applied, periodically, early in the subject's college career.

The TAT comprises a series of drawings and reproductions of paintings depicting ambiguous relationships between people, single individuals in ambiguous situations, or, in a few instances, landscapes in which no human figures are visible. Some of the pictures were especially designed for women or girls, some for men or boys, and some for both sexes and any age group. The pictures chosen were calculated to evoke certain themes, conflicts, or moods or to depict certain types of potentially conflictual relationships which most people have experienced.

The instructions generally call for the subject to tell, in response to each picture, a story that has a beginning, a middle, and an end or outcome. The subject is told that he may make any reference he wishes to the thoughts and feelings of the people he identifies in his stories. If, after the first card, the respondent has not told a story but described the picture, or has failed to include one of the component parts of the narrative, the instructions are repeated, with reference to what was omitted. No other directions are given during the test, and responses to the testee's questions are noncommittal. The test administrator writes down verbatim the stories offered by the subject or, in some instances, electronically records them for later transcription.

The entire set is rarely administered. Rather, a preselection of five to fifteen pictures is made either in terms of the administrator's standard procedure or on the basis of suspected problem areas in the subject's life. After the subject has responded to all of the cards selected, the test administrator may conduct an inquiry in which he attempts to induce the subject to repair omissions, offer clarifications and embellishments, and generally express any second thoughts on his interpretations.

As with the Rorschach test and many other projective devices, there is no standard procedure to which all psychologists adhere for use of the TAT. Many practitioners see merit in doing an inquiry after every picture, while still others find it convenient to use TAT pictures merely as an inducement to the client to describe his own personal problems.

An example of the use of the TAT as an assessment device is the picture, almost always presented first, of a boy seated at a table on which a violin rests. This stimulus characteristically evokes the dual themes of achievement and resolution of conflict with authority. Very frequently the boy is said to be forced by his parents to practice when he would prefer to be outside with his playmates. Following from this rather common definition of a problem a variety of story lines may be generated, each of which has a somewhat different implication: (1) The boy practices listlessly for the time required and then rushes out to play. (2) He sneaks out to play despite his parents' orders. (3) He is equally drawn to mastery of the instrument and to freedom from the demands of practice and tries to do his best in practice before joining his playmates at the earliest possible moment. As can be seen, it is possible to make inferences about the storytellers' attitudes toward authority, approach to resolution of conflict, and degree of internalization of parental aims.

Possible story outcomes are: (1) The boy comes to hate the violin and never plays as an adult. (2) He develops a modest competence which has recreational value and is pleased as an adult that his parents kept him at the task. (3) He discovers he has a real talent and goes on to be a virtuoso. One could infer that the first subject's life is governed by reaction to authority rather than by his own aims; that the second subject is a realist in the sense of trying to reconcile personal gratifications with external demands; and the third frees himself from realistic confrontation of interpersonal conflict by dreaming of glory. Depending, of course, on the richness of embellishment of the story outline and the degree of attention given to attitudes and motives of the boy and his parents, many other inferences could be drawn. It should, however, be kept firmly in mind that inferences drawn from the response to any one picture are merely hypotheses to be tested by reference to thematic content of the full range of stories offered by the subject. For example, one might conclude that the first subject was reactive to authority figures but quite comfortable and self-motivating in peer relationships.

Interpretation can be undertaken by meticulously tabulating story content through the use of one of the formal scoring systems based on the Murray "Need-Press" concept, and then by a process of analogical reasoning which assumes that elements dominant in the stories faithfully reflect characteristic resolutions of problems in real life. Alternatively, the familiar impulse-defense model can be applied to story content. The interpreter attempts to construct a picture of the subject's characteristic defensive maneuvers in response to impulses implicit in the story content. As is the case with other projective devices, an articulate, sophisticated interpreter can draw inferences from TAT stories which are little short of miraculous both to the uninitiated and to more pedestrian practitioners. Regrettably, until the criterion problem is solved, these masterful productions, however convincing they may seem, are based more on personal qualities of the interpreter than on a particular program of training or known correlations between story content and structure and verifiable characteristics of the subject.

THE CLINICAL INTERVIEW
AS A DIAGNOSTIC TOOL

Despite the large number of projective and psychometric tests available, and despite the steady accumulation of data suggesting that interviews may not be truly reliable indicators, when asked which technique for the assessment of personality they would retain if limited to only one, most clinicians choose the clinical interview (Kelly and Fiske 1951). It is not surprising that this is so, for in the hands of the skilled practitioner the interview is a highly flexible instrument that permits economical investigation in breadth and depth of symptoms and life history.

Nevertheless, the ease with which the presentation of one's self to another can be distorted, disguised, or misleading is well known (Goffman 1961). We are aware, for example, that even chronic schizophrenics can manipulate and control the impression they make in an interview; within limits they can appear to be sick or well depending on what is at stake. Braginsky and Braginsky (1967) report that if one questions the correctness of permitting a chronic schizophrenic patient to be on an open ward, he will present a justifying appearance of stability and rationality. And, if one suggests to a chronic schizophrenic that he is well and should go home (when he prefers to remain in the hospital), he will convincingly display evidence that he is sick and that the recommendation is ill founded.

If chronic schizophrenics can adapt their interview responses to their own ends, certainly less disturbed people are capable of an even greater degree of dissimulation and playacting to suit the occasion. Yet, the interview remains a favored diagnostic and therapeutic tool, even in circumstances where the interviewee has something to gain by being less than frank.

Each of our daily lives is filled with a succession of interviews that mark our interaction with others from morning till night. Such interviews (with a small "i") are the usual means by which we discover things about other human beings. When the Interview has a capital "I" and describes the interpersonal transaction between a client and a psychotherapist or diagnostician, it assumes a more formal and awesome aspect and seems to have a special and mysterious meaning.

Most often, the interview differs from the Interview in that the capital "I" suggests that a great deal is at stake—the prospective employee meets with the personnel director; the public figure interacts with the reporter; or the troubled human being seeks help from an expert. The Interview in diagnosis and therapy is in many respects like a scenario for a play, in which the stage setting is described only in broad outline, the roles are given titles (therapist-diagnostician and troubled client), but the lines of dialogue are missing. The actors are free to improvise as the feeling moves them at the moment in response to the stimulus each provides to the other (Danskin 1955; Strupp 1958; Howe and Pope 1962).

The diagnostic interview differs as the cast of characters changes and as each of the participants brings to the setting a unique set of expectations, anticipations, experiences, feelings, and personal problems and needs. Since no two interviews can follow an identical course, this diagnostic tool must be used artfully as well as scientifically. Whatever level of skill the interviewer achieves, there are certain inevitable impediments to his gaining an even reasonably complete knowledge of the interviewee's beliefs, values, attitudes, and life circumstances. Chief among these are the previous life experiences that shape the perceptions of the two participants in a diagnostic interview and therefore strongly influence the content and character of their transaction.

Of the two participants, the professional diagnostician is presumed to be free from the distorting influence of his past experiences in interacting with the patient. He reacts to the patient differently than he would to his friends, colleagues, or family. As a part of his professional training he is taught to respond *professionally* rather than *personally* to how the patient acts or what the patient tells him. Many therapists obtain personal psychotherapy as an aid to freeing themselves of obtrusive areas of hypersensitivity in interpersonal relationships which may interfere with their professional role.

The therapist is, moreover, protected by his role. He need not respond to intrusive questions of his patients but, by definition, has social sanction to inquire into any area of his client's life. There is thus a considerable asymmetry in status, power, and privilege between the patient and the professional interviewer (Frank 1961). The client usually accepts unequal status as one of the conditions of receiving help, and he has usually decided that in some important respects he is less capable than his interviewer or he would not be seeking help in the first place.

In most other relationships between a client and a professional (such as an architect, physician, lawyer, tax consultant, or repairman), the asymmetry in status is limited to the skills associated with the particular service being rendered and, therefore, is no great threat to the client. But in the mental health professions there is no area of the client's current and past life that is closed to scrutiny and evaluation. The client, whether he likes it or not, is expected to lay himself on the line as a person. Hence, it is not surprising that a great majority of clients initially offer the interviewer a neatly packaged set of symptoms that will, they hope, be relieved without necessitating total involvement of all aspects of their personality. The failure of many mental health specialists to appreciate this crucial difference between their expectations and the expectations of their clients undoubtedly contributes in part to the less than encouraging statistics on dropouts from mental hygiene clinics.

The Roles of the
Participants

If a patient expects to present not himself but only his symptoms and problems, he will not anticipate being personally involved in the interview transaction. However, since he needs relief from his symptoms and sees the interviewer as instrumental to this end, he must be alert to ways in which he should perform properly to induce the expert to help him. Ordinarily, this involves opening up areas of thoughts and feelings that may seem to be only tenuously related to his problems.

The patient has not been trained to control his reactions to the interviewer nor has he, in all likelihood, spent much time assessing his values, beliefs, attitudes, or emotional reactions, either to the therapist or to others. Thus, while he intends to relate to the interviewer in such a way as to enhance the probability that his problems will be resolved, he may initially misjudge what is appropriate—that is, appropriate from the standpoint of the interviewer or the expert observer.

For example, if the patient has had the experience of growing up with parents who are harsh, critical, and frequently angry, then he may expect the interviewer to be of a similar temperament. He may then be guarded, cautious, and noncommittal to ward off the anticipated harsh, critical attitude of the interviewer. If significant people in the patient's life could be moved only by extravagant displays of feeling and emotion, then the patient may attempt to appear sincere to the interviewer by producing emotional outbursts of the kind that have always elicited desired responses in the past.

Speaking broadly, whatever generalizations the patient has made from his life experience about those from whom he must seek help, he will bring to the diagnostic interview. These perceptions and expectations are like a complicated filter that allows only some communications and certain associated feelings to pass while it prevents others from getting through at all. What the client reveals and the manner in which he reveals it is an index to the sources of security and insecurity that mark the recurrent transactions with others through most of his life. It is the task of the diagnostician-interviewer to create an atmosphere of acceptance that will permit the client to somewhat relax these patterns of behavior.

The interviewer's job is a delicate one, for he must study his own reaction to the patient's manner of relating to others as well as the reactions of the patient. He must ask himself questions such as the following:

Is the patient hostile and angry, or am I more than ordinarily vulnerable today to his irritable manner? Is the patient really inarticulate and unresponsive, or am I dominating the interview and allowing him no real opportunity to talk? Is this young woman really as helpless and exploited as she says, or am I inclined to want to defend her because she is appealing and pretty? Is this older man trying to make me feel incompetent, or am I reacting to him as I have sometimes reacted in the past to paternal figures?

The competent interviewer continually monitors the feelings the client evokes in him at the same time that he tries to behave in such a way as not to evoke undesirable responses on the part of the client, responses such as distrust and resentment. Many diagnosticians, in meeting this problem, adopt a manner of professionally detached, protective neutrality which gives them an appearance of being distant and uncaring. The most gifted diagnosticians, on the other hand, are genuinely responsive and allow themselves to be sympathetically and empathetically involved in the client's difficulties but not to a degree that prevents their discerning accurately what is occurring in the transaction. This ability to be both involved and detached at the same moment is indeed a technical skill that is difficult to develop. It is, however, a skill that is the result of training, not a divine gift.

The perceptive interviewer depends not on words alone but also on what is silently communicated by facial expression, gestures, and bodily posture (Auld 1961; Boomer 1963; Ekman 1964). In addition, the experienced clinician is just as alert to what is *not* said, *how* something is said, and *when* something is or is not said as he is to the content of the client's message.

In drawing meaning from the interview, analysis may proceed at more than one level. There is, first of all, a record of what the client said—the manifest content. Second, there is an association of themes or emotion-laden elements in the client's communications. This association often leads to conclusions different from those the client wishes consciously to convey—the latent content. Finally, these two levels of data are fitted to a model of personality functioning that permits some further, albeit cautious, conclusions about the meaning of the client's responses to the interviewer in the clinical assessment situation.

It should be evident that the clinical interview not only provides essential diagnostic data but also offers a basis for making a formulation which attempts not only to identify and classify the particular pattern of symptoms described or exhibited by the patient but also to arrive at some conclusions regarding the nature and history of the overload on the personality. More often than not, in making such a formulation the interviewer draws on the personal history of the patient to identify those patterns of behavior, displayed early in life, that were minimally adequate to meet environmental demands in some prior period but are inappropriate at present.

The problem faced by even the most skilled interviewer in interpreting a client's current problems from the perspective of his life history is that, while he knows very well what kinds of human problems generate symptoms and the range of human responses to stress, it is often difficult to associate properly a set of stresses with the particular symptoms reported. For this reason, the informed, experienced clinician covers as wide a range of data as he can in the time available and suspends judgment until all of the data are in.

Guidance-Cooperation and
Mutual-Participation Approaches

There are two major approaches to diagnostic interviewing. The first, which derives from medical tradition, is focused not on the patient but on his symptoms. The intent of this method is to explore thoroughly and systematically all areas of the patient's history that accumulated professional experience has indicated may be the source of his complaints. The interviewer using this method tries to uncover an objective picture of a pattern of symptoms rather than to develop a relationship with the patient. He takes the initiative in asking concise, relevant questions to which he expects the interviewee to respond with concise, relevant answers. This is sometimes referred to as the *guidance-cooperation* model of clinical interviewing, and it has the advantage of enabling the interviewer to achieve broad, rapid coverage of life history data. By implication, of course, this approach suggests that the client has nothing to contribute but close attention to the questions and cooperation in giving the most accurate answers possible. Around this latter issue critics of the question-and-answer technique generated a radically new concept of interviewing which is often termed the *client-centered* or *mutual-participation* model.

The exponents of the mutual-participation approach contend that events or sequences of behavior in a client's life lack meaning unless one knows how they were experienced and how they relate to other events in his life (Rogers 1961). Moreover, they assert, the only way one can come to understand an incident, symptom, or problem in the context of an individual's life experience is to encourage him to talk freely, without strict regard for relevance or factual content.

It is assumed that, given this freedom and encouragement, the client will spontaneously reveal what most concerns him and will make these disclosures in such a manner as to demonstrate clearly how these focal problems influence his life. The information thus gained is believed to be more valid, since the atmosphere in which it is gathered lets the client feel that he, rather than his symptoms, are important to the interviewer. At its best, the interview can communicate to the client his importance as a person. At the same time, the spontaneous discussion covers the range of information necessary for a tentative diagnostic formulation.

Skill in conducting such an interview requires that the clinician be so thoroughly familiar with the types of information needed that he does not need a checklist to guide him. As the client freely describes and interprets his problems in the light of his life situation, the interviewer can readily obtain much of the data he needs (although not usually in an orderly sequence) and reliably infer from allusions and contextual remarks much additional information. To the fully persuaded client-centered practitioner, obtaining information leading to a diagnostic statement is never an acceptable objective in an interview. To diagnose a client is to destroy the feeling of mutual participation which, in turn, engenders the empathy and positive regard between persons judged to be essential in a helping relationship.

RELIABILITY AND VALIDITY
OF DIFFERENT TECHNIQUES

In summary, criteria such as demonstrated validity and reliability of techniques (techniques, moreover, that can readily be taught) point to measurement of intellectual functioning as far and away the most important contribution of psychologists to clinical assessment in the field of mental health. Perhaps a majority of clinical psychologists would disagree and would argue, instead, for the benefits conferred by the many, widely used projective devices. It is quite possible to see the merits of this position, but it requires a rather subtle and elaborate defense involving considerable speculation. Tests of intellectual functioning need no such defense, because compelling demonstrations of their efficacy in reliably distributing adequate samples of subjects over a continuum defined by consensually validated external criteria have been given.

To understand the contribution of psychological tests, one must recognize that insecurity is endemic in any well-run mental health institution. If all patients were treated alike, without regard for their individual histories and their unique array of potentialities (as is often the case in an institution with primarily custodial aims), then all concerned could be free of anxiety as long as established routines of minimum maintenance were carefully observed. However, most mental health professionals, out of humanistic concerns, wish to make the best possible use of a patient's individual capabilities, consistent with the limitations imposed by his condition. However, there are no consistent, external frames of reference against which to measure the adequacy of their judgments. In such circumstances, it is characteristic of humans to form mutual security pacts in which consensual agreement as to the appropriateness of a particular attitude toward or program of treatment for a patient becomes the mandate for action.

Thus, in a conventional mental health team comprised of psychiatrists, social workers, and a clinical psychologist, the last is often a key figure in solidifying consensus regarding the diagnosis and proper treatment of a patient. Characteristically, patients referred for psychological testing present equivocal signs and symptoms, or they present complicated problems of management. The psychologist, with his tests, is credited with being an objective and impartial witness whose data can effectively resolve many clinical dilemmas. Ideally, the clinical psychologist's most valuable contribution might be the opening of areas of inquiry, the generation of alternative hypotheses to explain observed behavior, and the stimulation of a broader and deeper examination of a client's life. Unfortunately, in any clinical decision-making situation, the alternatives for action are very limited, while the facets of a client's problems in living are numberless. In this paradoxical sense, the potential values of a psychodiagnostic examination are also its liabilities.

Psychologists, particularly those in training, are often dismayed by the apparent casualness with which much of the information in their elaborate reports is treated in clinical conferences. What they fail to observe is the eagerness with which their judgment is greeted on the one or two controversial issues in a case. Similarly, the reaction to a psychiatric intake report or a social worker's family history is also likely to be governed less by its depth or insight than by its cogency in respect to resolving uncertainty about the most desirable treatment for a patient.

Earlier in the chapter we raised the question of whether the well-developed art of clinical assessment of psychiatric disorders can be converted into a technology. The answer is that it probably cannot. A diagnostic technology established within the framework of the scientific method has certain necessary characteristics. A sine qua non is the capacity of all appropriately trained individuals to define the pathological condition under consideration so accurately that by following certain prescribed steps all can agree that the condition exists in some degree or does not exist. This step has manifestly not been achieved in psychiatry or clinical psychology. Were this step achieved, several other requirements would also have to be met. The most important of these would be substantial agreement on the observations from which a diagnostic statement is generated.

That is, even if there were consensually validated conditions to diagnose, agreement would still be needed on the particular set of responses to the diagnostic instruments that were clearly associated with particular diagnostic categories. Moreover, it would remain to be demonstrated that suitably qualified practitioners could be trained to identify the particular patterns of response associated with these diagnostic categories.

The fundamental reason for the apparent insolubility of the criterion problem in psychological assessment is the fallibility of human judgment of other humans. *My* son may be brilliant; *your* son is studious; and *his* son is a grind. *My* daughter is delightfully spontaneous; *your* daughter is rather flamboyant; and *his* daughter is semidelinquent. It is not a long step from the casual, gossipy observations of everyday life to the consequential observations of the behavior of patients. *My* patient is sometimes confused; *yours* has an obvious thought disorder; *his* is clearly schizophrenic.

Quite apart from the position of the observer, the meaning of communications regarding client's condition is often diffuse if not obscure. One study (Siskind 1967) of the degree of common understanding among clinicians of the meaning of a list of key words used in communication about psychiatric patients revealed an average agreement of about 50 percent. There is probably even less agreement on the meaning of many common words used in everyday conversation, but this difficulty is usually overcome by denotation and redundancy. To qualify as a technical language, word usage in clinical psychology and psychiatry should have a much higher level of consensus.

Still another and perhaps the major source of difficulty in demonstrating correspondence between responses to projective tests and observed behavior in other contexts lies in the human's unique capacity for disguise, duplicity, and deception. Observations deriving from projective tests may be absolutely valid: if characteristic X is prominently reflected in the subject's test protocol, it is actually to be found in his personality. However, finding characteristic X in the subject's behavior may be extremely difficult. A characteristic that would attract unfavorable attention or result in loss of status or self-esteem may be expressed surreptitiously. It could be expressed mainly in unspoken fantasy supported by selected readings or movies with a particular theme. It could be expressed only in partnership with a coconspirator who is allowed expression of some unacceptable characteristic in his personality in exchange for toleration of the subject's. It could be expressed as a component of perfectly ordinary behavior which, however, has a special meaning for the subject. It could be expressed openly only at wide intervals in situations that serve as a cover or excuse.

In short, twenty witnesses who know the subject very well might quite honestly deny ever seeing evidence of characteristic X. Parenthetically, I have never seen a newspaper account of a sudden, violent criminal act by an ordinary citizen in which friends, family, and neighbors did not profess astonishment. Partly, this is a consequence of a conspiracy in which most members of a social community participate. To protect themselves against confronting difficult and unpleasant interpersonal situations, they dismiss or normalize lapses from expected behavior. Nevertheless, the ordinary citizen can appear to be quite ordinary to his associates for long periods of time, while carrying within himself a kind of psychic time bomb which can explode under certain circumstances. Given this capacity for concealment, it is little wonder that the task of developing usable criterion data proceeds slowly.

DIAGNOSTIC TRAINING

If training in the clinical use of projective devices cannot be technical because of the criterion problem, it can, nevertheless, be formal, and there is very strong social endorsement of formal training even in professions and skills which by their very nature can never be scientific. It is quite impossible to set out to train a good lawyer, a good clergyman or, for that matter, a good executive. Role performance in these and many other occupations cannot be defined by reference to well-established external criteria. Nevertheless, most responsible people agree that lawyers, clergymen, and high-level executives should have a demanding educational experience before they practice.

A formal education provides familiarity with a body of customs, theories, practices, and substantive knowledge which taken together are a useful, if nonspecific, foundation for working with certain kinds of human problems in certain kinds of settings. A clinical psychologist's formal training, likewise, provides him with a sophisticated framework within which he can conduct a disciplined examination of human behavior. The clinical psychologist is also trained to be systematic in his use of data. He is taught where to look for relevant information and, to a degree, is given instruction in what use to make of it. However, the instructor cannot tell the student exactly how to apply data to a clinical

problem any more than a professor of law can tell a student exactly how
to win a case in court. He can demonstrate, discuss assessment in general
terms, suggest alternative formulations to those offered by the student,
point to distorted logic or to the intrusion of wishful thinking into an
interpretation, and make certain that a student builds a case study in
a logical way. All of these exercises can serve to channel the natural
abilities of the gifted practitioner and enhance the competence of the
person with modest endowments.

At this stage in the development of clinical psychology, training generally produces relatively sophisticated professionals deeply committed
to a study of the psychology of the functioning, whole person. Such a
product is socially valuable, but it is not the same thing as producing
a scientist with a body of validated, technical knowledge available to him.

NEUROPSYCHOLOGY AND
PSYCHOMETRICS

By contrast with the complex role of practicing clinicians, the contributions of neuropsychologists and specialists in psychometrics can be succinctly stated. This is not because their work is less significant but because
it is relatively unambiguous in both intent and procedure. Essentially,
the task of the neuropsychologist is to determine whether patterned
deficits in performance on a wide range of psychological tests can be
reliably associated with evidence of particular types of damage in
particular areas of the brain. Included among the deficits studied are the
aphasias, since the use and comprehension of language is so centrally
important to normal human functioning.

Standard neurological examinations have long incorporated sets of
questions designed to tap psychological deficits in patients with suspected
brain injury or disease. Clinical estimates of orientation (time, place, and
person), recent memory, remote memory, retention and immediate recall,
counting and calculating, general knowledge, abstract thinking, insight,
judgment, reliability, and language usage were part of the neurologist's
routine approach to diagnosis before clinical psychology existed as a
recognized profession. Consequently, the contribution of the psychologist
has been principally that of systematizing measurement of deficiencies
in these various areas of functioning through the development of specialized tests or the application of specialized scoring keys or interpretive
schemes to widely used standard tests of functioning on verbal and nonverbal tasks.

The psychologist is faced with two related problems in the construction of instruments to measure brain function. The first is to devise means of reliably differentiating the subset of patients with actual brain damage from a general population of respondents whose brains are intact. The second is to reliably differentiate functional deficits in performance that accompany neurotic and psychotic conditions from those that are the result of demonstrable brain damage or disease. A problem arises in the first instance because on virtually any measured performance it can be anticipated that a random sample of the general population will distribute itself over a considerable range. Likewise, brain-damaged individuals will distribute themselves over a range. As an illustration, performance on a test of recent memory—a critical function often impaired in the brain damaged—will show some apparently healthy individuals scoring poorly on the test and some patients with known organicity scoring fairly well. This reflects (1) that interpretation of tests of performance found useful in diagnosing brain damage are complicated nearly as much by the factors of education, background experience, motivation, and test-taking attitude of the subject as any other psychological instruments; and (2) that the effects of brain damage on test performance can be mitigated or exaggerated by the effect of personality factors.

The two problems noted above are susceptible to solution because criteria of the validity of the neuropsychologists' tests—that is, tangible evidence of brain damage or disease established by means external to the psychodiagnostic test procedures—are far less equivocal than those with which clinical psychologists typically deal. In this connection it should be noted that severe brain damage affects performance in ways that are almost unmistakable, regardless of the background of the patient or his efforts to compensate. Thus, it is only in the range of mild and moderate organicity that systematic studies must be made in order to isolate the effects of the patient's background and motivation. Actually the problem of taking account of deliberate efforts of the patient to disguise his disability is not a difficult one, unless social and occupational adjustment are used as a test. A person with mild to moderate brain damage will almost certainly reflect some loss of capacity on a formal test. At the same time, however, a strongly motivated, resourceful person who is unwilling to relinquish the level of achievement reached prior to his injury or illness can go a long way toward compensating for his loss. In particular, recovery of proficiency in speech after a cerebrovascular accident or trauma depends very heavily on the amount of determined effort put forth by the patient during the period of retraining. Likewise, mitigation of memory loss can depend upon the willingness of the patient to accept his reduced function, his ingenuity in devising memory aids, and his skill in reducing his exposure to situations requiring accurate recall without the use of notes. It should, perhaps, be noted in passing that psychologists have made significant research contributions in the area of rehabilitation as well as in the assessment of brain damage.

The two related, continuing problems with which neuropsychologists must cope are the degree of sophistication of validated knowledge regarding brain function and the state of the technology of test construction. As indicated above, early work in measurement was concerned with developing somewhat more precise tests of functions customarily reviewed by neurologists in their diagnostic studies. Deficits in these functions in the brain injured had been established on a purely empirical basis, and relatively little attention had been devoted to building tests consonant with well-supported theories of brain function.

The resolution of these related problems in neurophysiological theory and psychometry will not, of course, resolve the major dilemma inherent in the psychodiagnosis of brain impairment—the accurate determination of a baseline or index of pretraumatic performance of a brain-damaged individual. It is usually only by chance, and in a very small number of cases, that there exist adequate records of psychological tests reflecting a patient's level of functioning prior to being afflicted with disease or injury. For this reason, in the development of tests of organicity, much attention was given to the discovery of functions that are relatively well retained in spite of brain damage. In general, long-established and persistently rehearsed abilities are retained better than others. Thus, such abilities as power of vocabulary, general knowledge, and practical judgment are said to "hold" when brain damage occurs, while abilities such as recent memory, rate and retention of new learning, and abstract reasoning are said to deteriorate. Therefore, degree of brain impairment was traditionally judged to be reflected in a ratio of scores on "hold" and "don't hold" tests. If there was a virtual identity in the two sets of scores, the case for brain damage was weakened; if the "don't hold" scores were substantially lower, the probability of the existence of brain impairment was greatly enhanced.

This rather cumbersome approach has been only indifferently supported by empirical evidence, and the rationale for it has been challenged on theoretical grounds. The most telling criticism is directed at its overly simplistic conception of brain function which, in turn, is seen as contributing to the equivocal empirical support. The brain is a complex, dynamic organ that responds in complex ways to disease or injury. Thus, the hope that a single test diagnostic of brain impairment could be discovered is unrealistic. Even if such a test were available, it could not tell us what it is important to know from a functional standpoint. In the simplest terms, we know that the brain is part of the physiochemical system of the body and is therefore subject to changes in overall efficiency depending upon the general condition of the body's health. Stress in the form of fatigue, disease, nutritional deficiency, or severe psychological conflict may be reflected in impaired functioning of the brain just as certainly as will reduced blood supply with advancing age or actual injury to the brain tissue. Thus, on a theoretical basis, it is reasonable to assume a wide range of intra-individual variation in function—a consideration that receives only scant attention in psychological testing. Although most examiners routinely report an estimate of how truly a patient's test performance reflects his optimal functioning, the usual basis of such a judgment is the psychologist's gross assessment of the subject's willingness and ability to cooperate with the examination procedures employed.

It is now believed that the functions of the brain can best be conceptualized as a complicated central control for an elaborate feedback system. As such, the brain not only receives sensory data, transforms them for purposes of storage and retrieval, and sets in motion appropriate responses to environmental demands, but it also actively monitors and controls what data it will receive—including various kinds of stimuli that originate internally rather than in the external environment. It is now, moreover, suspected that the process of transforming the data to be stored differs, depending upon the type and utility of inputs; for example, long-term memory may result from enduring chemical changes while short-term memory may represent transient changes in electrical potentials.

It follows that disease or trauma may affect the several control functions differentially. It is now believed that the brain is not merely damaged or undamaged, but that it can be damaged or diseased in any number of ways, each of which has a somewhat different implication for function. Psychologists have scarcely begun to investigate just how these much-elaborated conceptions of brain function can be utilized to modify the assessment of brain damage through the use of psychological tests. It seems inevitable, however, that researchers will develop a more sophisticated approach than that embodied in the "hold–don't hold" hypothesis and that the fruitless research for a single, reliable test of organicity will be abandoned.

These researchers may take their inspiration from J. P. Guilford (1957), who has offered a tentative three-way organization of intellectual tasks that vastly enlarges the number of distinct facets of brain function that can be identified and related to known damage. Guilford hypothesizes 5 types of mental operations—memory, cognition, convergent thinking, divergent thinking, and evaluation—each of which has a content (figural, symbolic, semantic, and behavioral) and a product (units of information, transformations, and implications). Five operations multiplied by 4 content categories multiplied by 6 products yields to a structure of intellectual functioning with 120 different cells, each of which could be theoretically represented by an intellectual test.

Although the system is still under development and Guilford has matched only about 50 cells with tests, the elegance of the scheme reflects how narrow thus far has been the approach of clinical psychologists and neuropsychologists to the task of assessing intellectual functioning. Clearly, whether it is Guilford's scheme or some other, what is required is a wide array of tests of narrow band-width and high fidelity that capture faithfully each of the many complex functions of which the brain is capable and which it is regularly called upon to perform. As progress is made in this direction, it may then be possible to discern interdependencies and hierarchies of function.

At present, clinical psychology is lagging badly in its task of converting experimental findings on brain function into useful applications. There has been little advance in recent years over the crude empiricism of the organic batteries, some of which have been in use almost fifty years without substantial change.

If we were to separate the problem of measuring brain function from that of diagnosing gross pathology and conceptualize it as an important dimension of developmental psychology, then many existing difficulties in research and application would be obviated. We might, for example, obtain periodic measures throughout childhood and early adulthood which would provide not only baseline data against which to evaluate later losses with advancing age or injury but also a basis for studying intra-individual differences under varying degrees of physiological or psychological stress. The general problem we should be investigating is efficiency of function under a wide variety of circumstances, one subset of which would be demonstrated disease or trauma of the brain.

FACTOR ANALYTIC
TECHNIQUES

Factor analysis, a field in which Guilford has also made original contributions, is simply a mathematical device for simplifying the relationships between a complex display of variables. In effect, physicians who discover syndromes of symptoms that reliably point to a particular disease are intuitive factor analysts. They start by noting that, in a category of patients with one pronounced symptom, some other symptoms are regularly concurrent, while others may or may not be present. If the cluster of symptoms discerned is always associated with certain post-mortem findings, then the astute observer may have the honor of having a disease named after him. However, since psychiatry and clinical psychology lack anything comparable to a postmortem for the functional disorders, there is no effective way for the practitioner to sharpen and refine his intuitive judgment and clinical observations regarding classification of his patients.

The psychologist trained in psychometry is at least able to apply a well-developed methodology to this problem. It should be understood that the psychologist brings no magic, for he is no more able than the psychiatrist to bridge the basic discontinuity between biologically based medicine and behaviorally based psychiatry. But he can make more systematic observations and apply statistical techniques to abstract from his observations a taxonomy that meets certain specifications regarding the degree of independence of the categories identified. The psychometrician is likely to identify himself with the problems of the administrator of mental health institutions rather than with the psychotherapeutically oriented practitioner. That is, he is attempting to devise reliable instruments that can be employed economically in classifying large populations of patients. The actuarially based classification systems are designed to help the administrator in reaching decisions he is called upon to make.

Although the statistical procedures remain substantially the same in each case, psychometricians have used several points of departure with respect to basic data. For example the Minnesota Multiphasic Personality Inventory (MMPI), probably the most widely known test with a clinical flavor, was originally constructed of 550 items based on diagnostic cues used by psychiatrists (and on items from other inventories) and was designed to serve as a device for identifying patients falling in several conventional diagnostic categories, namely: (1) HS—hypochondriasis; (2) D—depression; (3) HY—hysteria; (4) Pd—psychopathic deviate; (5) MF—masculinity-femininity; (6) Pa—paranoia; (7) PT—psychasthenia; (8) Sc—schizophrenia; and (9) Ma—hypomania.*

Originally it was assumed that by systematically incorporating all cues conventionally used by a clinical interviewer, the MMPI could be made to serve as a reliable diagnostic device with great economies in

---

* The literature on the MMPI, because of its very wide use in clinics and hospitals as well as more generally as a personality inventory, is very large. For a discriminating selection of the most significant papers, the reader is referred to G. S. Welsh and W. Dahlstrom, eds., *Basic Readings on the MMPI in Psychology and Medicine* (Minneapolis: University of Minnesota Press, 1956).

professional time. While it has served this purpose in a rough way (the consensus is that while it can identify diagnostic groups with fair success [Guthrie 1950], it may be more prudent to use the instrument to identify individuals in a large group of patients who deserve additional study by other means), it very rapidly was converted by intensive research to use as a general personality inventory through profile pattern analysis and the development of a large number of specialized scoring keys. In the course of this modification in its application, the face validity of its constituent items became almost irrelevant, and its interest for us in this context is correspondingly reduced.

A somewhat better illustration for our purposes lies in the work of Maurice Lorr, who for many years has devoted himself to factor analytic studies of psychiatric symptomatology with the intent of isolating and identifying syndromes that are satisfactorily independent and reliable. Lorr's basic data collection device is the Inpatient Multidimensional Psychiatric Scale (IMPS), comprised of 75 brief rating scales.* From these scales 10 syndromes have been extracted (Lorr, Klett, and McNair 1963). Each of the syndromes listed below is characterized by a set of scales, from 5 to 11 in number, that identify a unitary pattern of behavior:

1. EXCITEMENT (EXC). The patient's speech is hurried, loud, and difficult to stop. His mood level and self-esteem are elevated, and his emotional expression tends to be unrestrained or histrionic. He is also likely to exhibit controlling or dominant behavior.

2. HOSTILE BELLIGERENCE (HOS). The patient's attitude toward others is one of disdain and moroseness. He is likely to manifest much hostility, resentment, and a complaining bitterness. His difficulties and failures tend to be blamed on others.

3. PARANOID PROJECTION (PAR). The patient gives evidence of fixed beliefs that attribute a hostile, persecuting, and controlling intent to others around him.

4. GRANDIOSE EXPANSIVENESS (GRN). The patient's attitude toward others is one of superiority. He exhibits fixed beliefs that he possesses unusual powers. He reports divine missions and may identify himself with well-known or historical personalities.

5. PERCEPTUAL DISTORTIONS (PCP). The patient reports hallucinations (voices and visions) that threaten, accuse, or demand.

---

* There are many other well-developed personality inventories, used mainly in schools and college counseling programs, which may occasionally have utility for screenng or research in psychiatric settings. The reader is referred to L. J. Cronbach, *Essentials of Psychological Testing*, 2nd ed. (New York: Harper and Brothers, 1960) for an authoritative commentary on test construction generally, and on well-constructed inventories in common use.

6. ANXIOUS INTROPUNITIVENESS (INP). The patient reports vague apprehension as well as specific anxieties. His attitudes toward himself are disparaging. He is also prone to report feelings of guilt and remorse for real and imagined faults. The underlying mood is typically dysphoric.

7. RETARDATION AND APATHY (RTD). The patient's speech, ideation, and motor activity are delayed, slowed, or blocked. In addition, he is likely to manifest apathy and disinterest in the future.

8. DISORIENTATION (DIS). The patient's orientation with respect to time, place, and season is defective. He may show failure to recognize others around him.

9. MOTOR DISTURBANCES (MTR). The patient assumes and maintains bizarre postures and he makes repetitive facial and body movements.

10. CONCEPTUAL DISORGANIZATION (CNP). Disturbances in the patient's stream of thought are manifested in irrelevant, incoherent, and rambling speech. Repetition of stereotyped phrases and coining of new words are also common.

It is now possible to take, as Lorr and his colleagues have, combinations of the 10 scales to identify categories of patients in a hospital population. These syndrome profiles are said to be related to ward assignments, conventional diagnostic categorizations, and obtrusive features of the patients' behavior. The advantage they have over conventional categories is that they are "clean"—that is, they reflect types painstakingly developed out of units of behavior that are well defined and can be reliably observed.

Thus, for example, in a sample of patients diagnosed as psychotic many would be diagnosed as paranoid type. However, this term in conventional clinical usage has different meanings for different clinicians. How much more functional it would be to use Lorr's system, which could reliably differentiate within this general and somewhat diffuse diagnosis at least four and perhaps more functionally important categories of patients.

In one study of a psychiatric population Lorr identified, among others, the following types (the numbers in parentheses refer to the ten categories delineated above): Excited-Hostile (1-2-3-10), Hostile-Paranoid (2-3), Hallucinated Paranoid (3-5-8), and Grandiose Paranoid (3-4-5). Of the patients in these categories, between 64 percent and 78 percent had been previously diagnosed simply as paranoid type. The attractiveness of the approach exemplified by Lorr's work is that each diagnostic category is logically coherent and tied to observable data that serve to define the type accurately and to distinguish it from other types. A ward staff, all of whom were familiar with the system, could communicate far more precise, useful information about the relevant behavior of a patient by applying syndrome score profiles than by any existing diagnostic scheme in common use.

Lorr's work is not the only thoroughgoing effort to apply contemporary statistical methodology to the problem of classification of psychiatric disorders. It is, however, exemplary of systems that attempt to retain the terms familiar to psychiatry yet give them more precise operational definitions. J. E. Overall (1962, 1963) and J. R. Wittenborn (1962) are two other psychologists well known for their contributions in the same area.

Another general approach to classification is, perhaps, more uniquely a contribution of psychology but is far less easy to apply in everyday clinical practice. This is systematic work designed to define psychopathology in terms of patterns of deficits along such standard parameters as cognition, perception, attention, reaction time, sensory acuity, learning ability, memory, and so on. Shakow (1945, 1963) many years ago undertook extensive research in this general area in his laboratory at Worcester State Hospital; more recently, Witkin (1954, 1962, 1965) and his associates have made conspicuous contributions, particularly in the areas of perception and cognitive style. Zubin (1958, 1962, 1963) in several papers has summarized contributions to what he terms a "biometric" approach to classification.

These related approaches are promising in so far as they serve to tie psychopathological conditions to highly reliable observations of functional deficits that may be construed as underlying clinical symptoms, a development that would bring psychiatric diagnosis conceptually closer to the rest of medicine. Unfortunately, however, the measures of various classical psychological functions correlate better with individual clinical symptoms than with recognized syndromes. Further, no one undertakes to treat a psychiatric patient by attempting to directly alter his perceptual skills, cognitive style, or eye-hand coordination. These psychological functions are often impaired by the patient's psychiatric illness, and they often improve with treatment, but the pattern of deficits is not by itself ordinarily seen as the psychiatric illness.

Thus, while psychologists must be credited with making exhaustive studies of the effect of psychopathology on basic psychological functions, it cannot be said that this research has been widely applied to clinical problems. Application, where it occurs, has come through the incorporation of some of these research findings into the construction of new clinical assessment devices and, more often, into interpretation of conventional tests.

COMMUNITY PSYCHOLOGY

Community psychology is a relatively new professional venture, concerned largely with delivery of conventional diagnostic and treatment services in somewhat unconventional settings. Conventional, widely used psychodiagnostic devices serve as well in these settings as elsewhere. A logical development of community psychology would be the creation of diagnostic devices that serve to locate a client in his social support system and identify problems arising out of his disarticulation with the community in which he lives.

Beginnings have been made in this novel approach to assessment, one example of which is the Community Adaptation Schedule (CAS), devised by Sheldon Roen and Alan Burnes (1966). Although still mainly a research instrument, it points the way to new dimensions of psychological assessment and to an area of fruitful collaboration between clinical and social psychologists.

A CASE DIAGNOSIS

Textbooks and casebooks illustrating the use of diagnostic tests in clinical practice are readily available. (Allison, Blatt and Zimet, 1968; Schafer, 1954; Rapaport, Gill and Schafer, 1945; Freeman, 1962.) However, in subsequent chapters we shall encounter a young woman, Ginny, as a patient in psychotherapy. Hence it would be instructive to consider how her suitability as a patient might be viewed from the perspective of a psychodiagnostic assessment.

Ginny is the daughter of Grace H. whose case history is presented in *The Quiet Furies* (McNeil 1967, pp. 47, 48, 49):

> Grace H. was not really my client, but she was the primary problem of the daughter who had asked me to see her. She was all the hypochondriacal mothers rolled into one whose potential heart attacks had produced generation after generation of guilty sons and daughters tied tightly to mother's apron strings. Grace was a controller, a manipulator, a manager, and a user of other people. It was as if she gained her life's strength by preying on other human beings. She had reduced her husband to a quivering mass of soft-spoken compliance, and she had whipped her children into line as effectively as a Marine drill instructor. Her training program was almost

perfect since it began in infancy and covered the lifetime of her children.

The daughter, Ginny, was nearly 26 years old and unmarried. She was engaged but, after her father died, she had twice postponed her marriage for fear that her mother's health would be affected in some unrecoverable and probably fatal way. Her fiancé was losing patience, and, between his urgings and her guilt and concern, the engagement period had become a running battle between them. Ginny—under pressure from her fiancé—finally asked her mother to come and see me and talk to me about her health. Grace was ready, willing, and eager. She had nothing to fear since she knew she was sick and if doctors disagreed with her, the only logical explanation was that they were wrong. Grace was starkly and madly in love with an extended audience of medical men who could barely write fast enough to record the full range of the ills she had experienced.

When Ginny quit her job and went to college, it was a time of family catastrophe. Grace H. knew all about "those radical professors" and the "beatnik" types she would be exposed to and insisted that Ginny call her twice a week and tell her how things were going. Ginny went to college and dutifully called home twice a week, but every phone call was like taking an emotional bath from which she emerged exhausted and limp.

As Ginny and I traced the outline of her life, I was at once puzzled by how rarely she mentioned the existence of her father and how brief and unrevealing those comments that she made tended to be. To hear Ginny talk would lead naturally to the assumption that her father had died or deserted the family some years ago. Emotionally, Ginny's father had done just that. He had deserted his post as male parent under a barrage of withering fire from his wife.

An interviewer would observe at once that Ginny is a well-dressed, well-educated, and well-mannered young woman who takes pride in her appearance. He might also observe that she holds herself rather stiffly and that her voice reflects tension. Nevertheless, her speech, while animated and somewhat pressured, reflects that she is well-organized, coherent, and in command of herself. Thus, within a matter of seconds he could reach the tentative conclusion that she is not so disturbed as to be judged psychotic. His conclusion regarding the degree of impairment would be tentative because some paranoid clients make an initially excellent appearance only to reveal a serious thought disorder when particular topics or significant relationships are mentioned.

From the content of her report on her problems, the interviewer would readily discern the intensity of her ambivalence regarding both her fiancé and her mother. He would also observe her greatly reduced capacity to make important decisions and act on them. While he could accept at face value her belief that her relationship with her mother is a major problem, he would be sensitive to indications that her difficulties with her mother are obscuring other areas of conflict of which she is partially or completely unaware or which she is deliberately concealing. If, for example, she had not mentioned her father, despite many opportunities to do so, he might draw this to her attention. Similarly, he might direct her attention to the fact that while she has told in great detail about her mother's demanding, interfering behavior, she has not commented on her possible contribution to the troubled relationship.

In an unobtrusive way, the interviewer would try to determine to what extent Ginny's capacity for work, for enjoying a normal social life, for making and keeping friends of both sexes, for engaging in recreational activities, and so on might be reduced by her emotional problems. He would also try to get a clear picture of her symptoms and the circumstances in which they seem to be exacerbated.

His conclusion would almost certainly be that Ginny seems to be a capable, basically well-integrated person with moderate to severe psychophysiological reactions, emotional instability, anxiety, and periodic depression stemming from the acute conflict over a marriage opportunity to which her controlling mother is opposed. Left unanswered by the interview but potentially discoverable from Ginny's psychological tests are emotion-laden attitudes regarding sex and marriage which lie outside of her conscious awareness. Not uncommonly one person accuses another of frustrating a plan which he wishes unconsciously not to carry out. It is sometimes easier to assign blame to another than to uncover and face one's own underlying conflicts. Ginny's charges against her mother, for example, may be a screen to hide her own distaste for heterosexual intimacy.

Since there is no indication whatsoever of organic brain damage or of any intellectual incapacity, the psychologist would probably not schedule tests of intelligence, memory, or concept formation. Since he is interested in thematic material having to do with Ginny's relationship with significant family members and her fiancé, he would choose a set of TAT pictures and, no doubt, administer the Rorschach Ink Blot test. From the latter, he would hope to discern any indication of underlying personality disorganization not evident in the interview and to identify unconscious sources of threat to her self-image along with characteristic patterns of defense against the emergence of these hidden fears into consciousness.

For administration of the TAT pictures, the examiner might well choose the following:

1. A boy sitting pensively with a violin before him on the table.
2. A farm scene with a young woman in the foreground, holding books in her arms, a young man working in the fields in the background, and an older woman in the middle distance looking on.
3. BM. A figure, ambiguous as to sex, huddled against a couch, with a revolver on the floor beside the figure.
4. A woman holding onto a man whose face and body are turned as if he were trying to pull away from her.
5. A middle-aged woman looking into a room through a half-opened door.
6. GF. A seated young woman looking back over her shoulder at an older man.
7. GF. A young girl holding a doll, looking into the distance as an older woman beside her is speaking or reading to her.
12 F. A strange old lady with a shawl grimacing behind a young woman.
13 MF. A woman, apparently nude, lying on a bed in the background while a young man stands facing away from her with his head buried in his arm.

Although there is no certainty that it will do so, each picture is designed to elicit certain thematic material. Thus, the psychologist assumes that pictures 1, 2, 5, 7 GF, and 12 F will evoke fantasies regarding her mother. He expects pictures 2, 4, and 13 MF to elicit heterosexual themes, while pictures 1 and 2 may tap Ginny's concerns regarding achievement. Picture 6 GF should generate fantasy regarding the father figure, and picture 3 BM may indicate the extent to which depressive affect is a factor in Ginny's problems.

Let us assume the following results: In response to picture 1, Ginny gives a conventional story about a boy being required by his mother to practice when he would prefer to be outside playing. He gives in but never enjoys music later in life. One sees nothing really new in this response but merely a reflection of the dependency-independency conflict with mother. Ginny gives in but tries to punish her mother by her visible withdrawal of interest from any project her mother sponsors.

In story 2, Ginny reflects a belief that marriage and personal achievement are incompatible. The girl in the picture is seen as being in conflict over continuation of her education and moving away to take a position in the city as against marrying a farmer and remaining in the country.

A secondary but familiar theme reflects the mother figure's objecting to her daughter's taking steps toward independence.

Ginny's response to picture 3 BM does reflect her having entertained ideas of suicide but sternly rejecting this solution to her problems. However, the fantasied outcome is one of grim endurance without pleasure. In her response to picture 4 one sees the intensity of Ginny's apprehension regarding the capacity of a marriage partner to protect her against her mother's control. She tells a story of a young wife who is deserted by her husband and must return home to face her family's scorn. The same general theme is evoked in response to picture 6 GF, where a father is seen as telling his daugter that he will not finance her while she seeks employment in a distant city because her mother objects to this.

Pictures 5, 7 GF, and 12 F also elicit themes reflecting the intense conflict with her mother and anger toward her, and picture 12 F touches off a fantasy that the old queen-mother plans to kill the princess in order to prevent her from taking the throne when she is 21. This is an indication of how malevolent the mother may have appeared to Ginny when she was a small girl and represents a deeply repressed fear. Finally, in response to picture 13 MF Ginny again pictures the male as weak and frightened—ready to abandon the girl with whom he has been having sex because she is ill and represents a burden.

While little emerges from the TAT that is absolutely new, Ginny's stories underline the intensity of her conflict with her mother and go on to indicate that a significant part of the problem is her underlying belief that she has nowhere to go. That is, if she goes through the pain of separation from her mother in order to marry, all she can look forward to is abandonment by a weak and faithless man.

The examiner noted that Ginny followed directions closely, worked hard to produce stories of quality, and reflected a reasonable degree of ease in dealing with emotion-laden material. All of these capacities would be favorable signs for recommending therapy.

The Rorschach inkblots, because they are stimuli with no intrinsic meaning, are thought to have the potentiality of tapping deeper aspects of personality than more structured tests. At the same time, the feelings uncovered may be free-floating in that they are not clearly tied to particular objects or events.

Ginny, we will assume, gave about 40 responses to the ten blots (half of which are black and white and half with color). We will further assume that with one or two exceptions the form-level of her responses was satisfactory—that is, in scrutininzing the blots, Ginny takes care that the area to which she is responding really resembles (with minor discrepancies) what she has in mind before she reports her perception. A

severely disturbed person may repeatedly report seeing forms which he
cannot justify in terms of shape, color, or shading. Alternatively, an ex-
aminee may be so fearful of self-disclosure that he is unwilling to report
seeing anything but a splotch of ink. Moreover, she was rather systematic
in her assessment of the blots and responded both to the entire blot and
to parts of it. The examiner, however, noted a certain grimness in her
manner and a reluctance to take any pleasure in her imagination. She
seemed to be performing because she was supposed to rather than because of any personal satisfaction.

Ginny seemed sensitive to and even irritated by the indistinct quality
of some of the blots and noted that many of the objects seemed "shrouded
in haze" or were merely "storm clouds." She responded slowly to the
cards with color, commenting that they were "pretty" but unlike any
colors of real objects.

On the first plate she reported seeing a "female figure" in the center
which was "indistinct" and yet "somehow in control of the other figures
in the blot." On the third plate she noted two figures of men "who are
trying to lift something but are too weak to get it off the ground." On
the fourth card she avoided the center and found some small figures
on the periphery of the blot. Finally, she noted "some boots" (in large
details at the bottom). She gave a banal response to the sixth card, and
on the seventh saw "two little girls doing a pretty little dance they have
been instructed to perform." Responses to the ninth card were sparse
because "it is hard to break it down and it does not mean anything as
a whole." Blot ten was "confusing because there is too much separation
between the different parts," but eventually she picked out a number
of small objects often seen by examinees.

Once again, nothing previously unsuspected emerged from Ginny's
responses to the Rorschach test. On the other hand, the test provided
extremely valuable confirmation of earlier judgments made on the basis of
the interview and the TAT, and some new information emerged. Confirmed was Ginny's basically well-integrated personality and her business-
like, cooperative approach to help-seeking. The focal conflicts already
identified were reflected in Ginny's responses, together with the mildly
ominous indication that her unconscious perception of her mother is
fraught with anxiety so intense that her capacity for reality-testing is
sometimes seriously compromised.

In summary, the psychodiagnostician would judge that Ginny is an
excellent prospect for psychotherapy. She could readily comprehend the
aims and methods employed; she would be patient and hardworking in
phases when progress might be difficult to discern; the dynamics of her
problems are reasonably well defined; and she has the ego strength

ecessary to sustain her in confronting anxiety-provoking unconscious
notives, impulses, and fears as they emerge.

Individuals without Ginny's qualities might be judged poor risks for
nost therapeutic approaches. A person of only average intelligence or
below, with relatively little experience in introspection, impatient for
results, impulsive and poorly controlled in problem-solving situations,
possessing a weak or fragmented ego, and having conflicts which are
difficult to define would be a doubtful candidate for psychotherapy.*

---

* When this book was already in page proof, Robert Holt, an articulate spokes-
man for the clinician in the debate on the validity of the clinical method published a paper that very effectively summarizes the issues (Holt, R. R. Yet
another look at clinical and statistical prediction: or, is clinical psychology
worthwhile? *American Psychologist,* Vol. 25, No. 4, 1970, 337–49). This article
should certainly be read by anyone interested in the problem of predicting
behavior from performance on psychological tests. Holt's arguments against
critics of the clinical method as a valid assessment technique merit as much
attention now as they did more than a decade ago (Holt, R. R. Clinical and
statistical prediction: a reformulation and some new data. *Journal of Abnormal
and Social Psychology,* Vol. 56, 1958, 1–12. Republished in E. I. Megargee
(ed.), Research in clinical assessment. New York: Harper & Row, 1966; also
in three other sources.) However, the definitive research he recommended then
and now has never really been undertaken by proponents of the clinical method.
Since the burden of proof seems to fall on the clinician, it is unfortunate that
for so many years those who are convinced of the efficacy of the ideographic
approach have elected to substitute assertion for empirical evidence. Holt's
own research (Holt, R. R. and Luborsky, L. *Personality patterns of psychiatrists.*
Vol. 1. New York: Basic Books, 1958. Vol. 2. Topeka, Kansas: Menninger Foundation, 1958) is, of course, a partial rebuttal to the charge that clinicians seem
to prefer abstract argument to demonstration.

The Practice of
Psychotherapy

One should have no doubts that the persistent engagement of intelligent perceptive practitioners with the complicated problems of clients have yielded some valid observations and much wisdom. The problem is that out of the welter of observations drawn from practice, it is difficult to know which are valid (and under what conditions) and which are not. The method of participant observation may be useful in raising questions and generating hypotheses regarding the therapeutic process but it is poorly designed for testing the validity of propositions. As a deeply involved participant, the therapist can scarcely avoid selective attention to only a small fraction of the events in his transactions with the patient and because he cannot assimilate all the information available he is prone to retroactive falsification. That is, his recall is likely to be shaped as much by what his theoretical views indicate should have occurred as by what actually happened.

Given this difficulty inherent in trying concurrently to be a therapist and a detached observer and taking account of the relative lack of fully documented evidence regarding the events comprising psychotherapy, leads one to a position of benign skepticism regarding the claims of practitioners. Psychotherapists, reasonably enough, *want* to believe the particular set of techniques they have mastered and espouse are effective. Consequently, they *do* believe they are effective, objective data to the contrary.

The practice of psychotherapy is extremely demanding precisely because the therapist's zeal to help is not equalled by his capacity to do so. If a therapist is to be of any help at all, however, he must to some legree control the normal anxiety each of us experiences when we enter, poorly equipped, into a complex, demanding, and consequential relationship. Most therapists control this anxiety by adopting a set of beliefs about human personality and how one can bring about useful changes in behavior. Armed with these organized beliefs, the therapist can proceed with considerable confidence to confront and respond forthrightly to the problems presented by his client. The client is reassured by his therapist's appearance of being comfortably in command of a technique for resolving the personal difficulties that have thoroughly baffled and irritated him. In this atmosphere of security, the client may be able to reassess himself and his circumstances and break out of his rigid, repetitive, self-defeating ways of trying to handle the overload on his capacity for adjustment.

If, in addition, a particular set of beliefs about human personality and psychotherapeutic practice held by a therapist appears to be confirmed by a client's improvement, the client, like the therapist, will become attached to and defend this set of beliefs. The possibility that twenty different therapists with twenty different sets of beliefs might also get positive results does not distress the client who has experienced improvement. Nor is a therapist immune to seeing himself as rather especially gifted if his clients express satisfaction with his services.

Only when the therapist shifts his role from that of clinical problem solver to that of scientist or critical commentator does he allow himself true detachment. Even then he may be less than scrupulously objective and may resist taking seriously any theorist who questions the basic premises on which he believes his therapeutic work is based. An exception may occur when a therapist becomes a convert to a new system that promises greater effectiveness while violating few of his previously held convictions.

Make no mistake, however, these unsupported convictions are necessary, even if the beliefs lack validity and contribute mainly to the sense of personal security the therapist communicates to the patient. This security becomes an active therapeutic ingredient. Ultimately, of course, one would hope to see the birth of a commonly accepted, well-articulated set of beliefs and practices fully supported by empirical evidence. This time, alas, is far off.

The fact that there exists a wide variety of beliefs and therapeutic practices that have been successful in the sense that they have generated a large measure of verbalized satisfaction for essentially the same kind of patients lends credence to the notion that these various approaches all have something in common. We can only surmise what all of these factors are. We have already mentioned the utility of any body of theory and set of related practices that enhance the security and reduce the anxiety

of therapists. We should also note that all one-to-one therapies provid
a mandate for self-disclosure by offering virtually complete confiden
tiality to the patient. Moreover, most therapists tend to be nonjudgmenta
in those areas in which most clients have experienced highly critical re
actions from others. Finally, having committed themselves to a costl
and time-consuming process, most patients may entertain the persisten
belief that they are the recipients not only of the skill but also of the
goodwill, friendship, and even affection of their therapists. Schofield
(1964) has advanced the interesting observation that many of the characteristics attributed to able psychotherapists are also associated with
good friends. Hence, he speculates, many clients are actually paying a
fee to purchase the commodity of friendship which they have been unsuccessful in acquiring in the ordinary course of living.

Earlier, in Chapter 1, we noted the particular kind of friendship af-
forded a client by a therapist. It has the advantage of being disinterested
(the therapist has no stake in any particular outcome of the relationship,
provided it seems to be toward rather than away from adjustment) but
the disadvantage (as the client sometimes sees it) of not involving ready
acceptance of the client's version of his problems. Moreover, the "natural"
friend may or may not respect confidentiality, while the therapist-friend
almost certainly will. Since all of these factors are more or less common
to all therapies, one is inclined to give them more weight than some other
interesting but unconfirmed speculations.

Given the benign, confidential "friendship" with a therapist, a client
may not only be freed to reassess his own values, thoughts, feelings, and
behaviors, but he is likely also to be more receptive to the values,
thoughts, and problem-solving devices that are either implicit in the
therapist's behavior or are explicitly introduced by him in accord with
his views on the conduct of psychotherapy. This conclusion is supported
by indications that a wide variety of therapeutic practices not only seem
to have equal success with similar categories of clients but also seem
to have a considerable convergence of procedures.

The various schools of therapy each identify certain techniques as characteristic of or necessary to their approach. However, since no school
can dictate or carefully regulate how a therapist responds in the myriad
situations that develop in the course of extended encounters with a
diverse sample of clients, carefully trained therapists try to follow taught
prescriptions when they are available and when they are not, do what
comes naturally or what seems a reasonable extrapolation from those
principles. Since therapists tend to have a great deal in common with
one another (such as culture, class, education, and career aims), the

)ehavior they display in therapeutic encounters not specifically delineated
)y their training is likely to be more alike than different.

Nevertheless, there is a diversity of personality characteristics among
therapists as in any aggregation of people. And these individual differences in experience, values, affective range, and philosophic outlook find
expression in therapeutic work. Some therapists are warm, friendly,
supportive, and relaxed emotionally, while others are rather cool, detached, thoughtful, and restrained. Some therapists have flexible and
relative moral values, while others are rather absolute and rigid. Some
therapists are energetic and active, while others are passive and sometimes weary. Some are highly intelligent and others a bit dull.

In some instances a therapist is drawn to a particular school because
its precepts and practices seem congruent with his personality. In other
cases, therapists are attracted to a course of training by its high prestige
and verbalize acceptance of principles and practices which, in fact,
they cannot rigorously follow because of their temperament and philosophic outlook. Many originators of well-defined schools of therapeutic
theory and practice proposed techniques and viewpoints compatible with
their own personalities, and their followers often converted these practices
and principles into rigid dogma. Freud, for example, was a scholarly,
highly moralistic, restrained individual who adapted comfortably to
social isolation. One can only conjecture what psychoanalysis might have
been if Freud had been an ebullient, self-indulgent, socially aggressive,
emotionally unrestrained person.

At any rate, such individual differences among students, coupled with
general cultural prescriptions that run counter to the principles of any
given school, make it difficult if not impossible to conduct research into
the relative effectiveness of various forms of practice. We never seem
to discover therapists who truly embody the theory and principles of
practice of a school, as its precepts and aims are stated. We always end
up comparing groups of therapists whose practices tend to be more alike
than different, despite differences in their training.

The most prominent reason for hypothesizing that there is more similar-
ity in the practice of therapists than might be supposed from their theoretical persuasions is that all psychotherapies (with the possible exception of
highly experimental procedures involving written or tape-recorded client
communications reviewed and answered by a therapist whom the client
does not meet) are conducted in the context of a certain kind of relationship. Although Bordin (1959), Snyder (1961), and Loevinger (1963)
all allude to the triteness and lack of specificity of this affirmation, the
work of Fiedler (1950, 1953), and Heine (1953) demonstrates that, even

though clients note differences in technique between practitioners of different schools, they react as much or more to qualities of the therapeutic relationship which are not taken specifically into account in training programs. Strupp (1955, 1959, 1960*a*, 1960*b*), in a long series of research reports, has likewise shown that similarities and differences among therapists do not necessarily coincide with similarities and differences in their training. That is, while therapists may be consciously preoccupied with intervention along the lines determined by their school affiliation, they engage in transactions that have meaning for clients in terms of dimensions such as warmth, distance, status, congruence, credibility, likability, interest, and trust. (See Goldstein, Heller, and Sechrest, 1966, pp. 73–145 for a thoroughly competent review of the relevant research literature.) Many observers believe that the therapeutic transaction occurs in these areas of often unwitting communication between therapists and patient. Although some of these features of the relationship are consciously and mutually reviewed as issues in the therapy, others are never explicitly dealt with.

Success in helping clients thus seems somewhat less dependent on what one does than on how one does it. This does not imply that all therapists are equally effective, or that the theory of therapy one adopts makes no difference. However, the importance of a theory may lie in the extent to which it impedes or enhances the development of certain qualities of a therapeutic relationship that are the active agents. Researchers now suspect, but have not confirmed, which of the several discernible aspects of a therapeutic relationship are most important for a favorable outcome. But we do not yet know very well how to train therapists to maximize those qualities believed to be beneficial. When this line of research begins to bear fruit, each of the current schools of therapy will probably prove to have contributed something of value to the ultimate product.

Perhaps because of this apparent convergence in practice, doctoral programs in clinical psychology, which collectively do more training in psychotherapy than any other single type of institution, have tended to become more and more eclectic in their teaching. Students are exposed to or seek out a variety of points of view, few are indoctrinated and thoroughly schooled in any one. Even though the basic premises of two theories may be diametrically opposed to one another, students tend to choose those facets of both theories that seem useful for treating or understanding a client. It is no heresy to some practitioners, for example, to apply psychoanalytic principles to formulate a client's problem while treating him non-directively in the style of Rogers. Neither is it seen as necessarily illogical to treat different patients, or even different symptom clusters in the same patient, with a variety of techniques drawn from widely different sources; desensitization is used with one, analytic interpretation with another, and rational-emotive techniques with a third.

Given this pronounced trend toward eclecticism and the accumulated evidence that therapeutic practices have always been more convergent than divergent, the reader might well ask why we should devote the subsequent chapters to presenting the most prominent of the organized theories of psychotherapy. The primary reason is that blind eclecticism is ultimately nonproductive. It does not lead toward the creation of better and more comprehensive theories but toward a bland, anti-intellectual, atheoretical pragmatism that robs the practitioner of any anchoring point. It should be remembered that psychotherapy is an application of psychological principles which are ultimately rooted in the theories and research of behavioral scientists. Whatever practical success a therapist may enjoy through using one set of techniques or another, the scientific status of his procedures rests ultimately on a reconciliation of them with what is confidently known about human behavior. At present, there are strongly competing views of what comprises "human nature," each of which has a measure of empirical support. Eventually one of these conceptions (or some reformulations incorporating two or more) will gain strong support from scientific research. When this time comes, psychotherapeutic theory and practice will be directly affected and only those techniques which are linked most closely with verified propositions regarding human behavior will be accorded scientific support.

Meanwhile, even today, most well articulated theories of psychotherapy are either implicitly or explicitly based on particular sets of premises regarding man's nature. One may not be able, currently, to demonstrate empirically to a casually eclectic student that mixing procedures drawn from a variety of schools is not productive. At the same time, it is certainly possible to demonstrate the logical inconsistency of, for example, using psychoanalytic and client-centered, non-directive principles interchangeably. Both may be effective (or ineffective) in a particular case because we have not yet grasped the more general theory under which both sets of techniques may be subsumed. From a theoretical view, however, they emerge from views of man which are almost diametrically opposed.

Influential theorists, around whom "schools of therapy" have developed, each entertain rather different images of man and their techniques of therapy are presumed to follow logically from these beliefs about "human nature."

For example, if one starts with the premise that man is a highly intelligent animal who nevertheless retains beastly, antisocial instincts, then the goal of therapy is to assist the client to accept and express these inherited sexual and aggressive impulses in such a way that he does not invoke social censure. If one tries to pretend that these instincts do not exist, he is likely, according to this school of thought, to be inhibited, fearful, anxious, and conflicted in relationships with others. An impulse denied does not cease to exist but continues to exert its pressure for expression. If one cannot acknowledge sexual or aggressive drives in situations where such behavior is acceptable these occasions become fraught with tension and confusion and avoidance or inhibition the only source of relief.

If, on the other hand, one ignores social constraints and attempts to do what he pleases, when he pleases, in any way he pleases, he will certainly be punished—either directly through physical attack, arrest, or imprisonment, or more subtly, and in some ways more painfully, by rejection and social isolation. The therapist who accepts this view of man takes a somewhat pessimistic view of his task, since the best he can do is to help the patient perform a more adroit balancing act between his instinctual demands and the social requirements of society. Ideally, the patient should fully accept his impulsive nature at the same time that he accurately assesses the benefits of a conforming social existence and should devise the best possible compromise between impulse expression and social constraint. How this delicate balancing act is to be achieved will be considered later.

One might, however, entertain a quite different basic premise—that man has no inherently antisocial instincts and that, given a suitable developmental learning experience, he will not only find a painless and conflict-free place in society but will derive considerable satisfaction from effective social performance. There is always the possibility that an individual might receive inadequate childhood instruction and learn behavior that is inconsistent with the expectations of others in his social milieu. If he is punished for what he thinks is a correct solution to a problem, he may become tense, confused, and uncertain. He may attempt, in an aggressive way, to make his solution work even when he is punished for both the incorrect answer and the aggression. Or he may try to avoid being confronted with the problem. If the problem has to do with a recurrent, important aspect of living, nothing short of complete withdrawal will work. Thus, the task of the therapist who takes this viewpoint may be to identify areas in which his client has had poor learning experiences and to pursue a course of retraining. The new approach to problem-solving should earn social approbation instead of failure and social disfavor and therefore enhance self-esteem.

A third premise for a school of therapy is that man has unique capacities for the development of all kinds of talents, among which the most important is simply the capacity to enjoy his human status and what this implies in the way of self-reflective experiencing. The ideal, and, perhaps, unattainable goal is that of being a fully functioning, completely actualized man. This goal cannot be the same for all men, since there are individual differences in endowment. However, it is assumed that each individual can know what is his quintessential self if the socially imposed restraints on knowing are removed.

Or one can take as a premise that man is born in conflict and pursues a life of perpetual ambivalence. It may be assumed that the fundamental conflict in man is between independency and dependency, between activity and passivity, or between union and autonomy. Man may be seen as continually torn between a need to actively seek new experience and to effectively master the problems he encounters and a need to be gently nurtured and free of the necessity for lonely struggle. It is assumed that an individual who ignores either of these basic needs will suffer tension and anxiety. Thus, the healthy person is one who both keeps his needs in sight and serves them as best he can, and the therapist's task is to help the client accept life's inescapable dilemma and maintain a balanced style of life. An individual seeks therapeutic help when he becomes acutely aware that he behaves and feels in ways foreign to his dimly perceived "real" self. The therapist provides a sympathetic, supportive atmosphere within which the client feels free to examine what is specious about his behavior and to uncover the self that is authentic.

There are many variants of these four basic premises about the nature of man, but they differ in details, not in essentials. Needless to say, there are also many variations in therapeutic strategy and tactics among practitioners who espouse any given view. Some of these will be identified in the chapters that follow.

What remains to be underlined here is the extent to which essentially identical therapist behaviors may serve all four of the therapeutic goals that are the logical derivations from these concepts of human personality. Therapists of all persuasions need to know in the client's own words why he is seeking therapy, what areas of his contemporary life are the most problematic, what the client has attempted in the way of solutions, and where these solutions went wrong. All therapists are interested in the client's feelings about himself and the important people in his life. Moreover, as they encourage the client to reveal his life situation fully and truthfully, most therapists are affectively neutral in their statements, warm and supportive in their manner, yet nonjudgmental in attitude. These may be the irreducible factors common to all therapies.

Psychoanalytic Psychotherapy

4

Within the memory of many people alive today, psychoanalysis, as a theory of personality and a method of treatment, has emerged from the atmosphere of contempt and anger that greeted Sigmund Freud's first formulations to a dominant position in the training centers for mental health professionals. It is interesting to conjecture just what it was in Freud's theory that his professional colleagues and informed laymen found repugnant. The physicians of the time were totally immersed in the rational view of the universe that flowered in the nineteenth century and were not prepared to comprehend the concept of irrational psychological causation in mental illness, to say nothing of certain physical disabilities. Physicians and laymen alike were appalled at talk of infant sexuality and unconscious motivation, and they were very reluctant to apply such ideas to their own personal or family life.

One has the impression, however, that what really rankled people was Freud's attributing to everyone the same set of nasty thoughts and lustful or aggressive impulses that had, up to that time, been identified exclusively with thugs, deviates, perverts, and the insane. The fact that psychoanalytic views were as abhorrent as they were to self-styled decent citizens suggests that Freud was all too correct for comfort. Laying hypocrisy bare is likely to evoke anger, and Freud was sweeping away veils never touched before. Prophets have become martyrs for lesser affronts than Freud forced upon the Victorian society of his time.

86

NEUROTIC SYMPTOMS IN
CONTEMPORARY AND
VICTORIAN SOCIETY

Some subgroups in our society have recently advocated that conventional constraints on behavior be cast off—particularly in the spheres of sexual behavior, property rights, work discipline, and drug usage. Indeed, some subgroups advocate rather deviate norms regarding the employment of aggression to achieve social goals while others abhor its use under any circumstance. Virtually all contemporary societies, of course, sponsor the use of force in war and police actions but are rather touchy about unauthorized, uncontrolled aggression. Many young people today are far from convinced that aggression gains dignity or utility as a problem-solving device whether sponsored by a government or by groups bent on revolution. In any event, it is not difficult today to find spokesmen for a viewpoint that apotheosizes impulses and advocates conflict resolution by removing social constraints.

Some believe this leads to a rather squalid moral position that totally compromises the possibility of a durable social existence. Others observe that, squalid or not, deviant groups that extol free expression of certain impulses are altering the normative standards of social existence and will have some considerable effect on the entire society. Nevertheless, the outcome will simply be a new set of constraints opposing unalloyed expression of impulse. In Freud's view, the so-called instinctual drives are timeless, mindless forces too disruptive to be the basis of social life.

Nowadays, we are less upset by the notion that all men may share a set of instinctual drives that must be curbed or allowed only modulated expression if we are to live comfortably with one another in a highly articulated society. We are not alarmed that in our dreams and fantasies we find evidence of wishes and impulses that are not part of our ordinary waking life. We are also alert to the psychopathologies of everyday life— the slips of tongue; the forgetfullness; the sudden, transient, unreasonable irritations or depressions; and the other small, self-defeating maneuvers that reflect a mental life outside of immediate awareness and seemingly beyond our control. This does not mean, however, that we are free of neurotic problems. Rather, it implies that the modal patterns of symptoms today probably differ from those of Freud's Viennese patients at the turn of the century.

In that day, middle class culture was restrictive and repressive in tone, the children were confronted with powerful moral imperatives that etched deeply the contrast between what one was supposed to feel, think, and do and the way life was actually lived. In the course of growing up, many children were made to feel intensely guilty and anxious about sexual and aggressive impulses and were, at the same time, in constant association with adults who obviously did not always practice what they sternly preached. In such an environment, impulses were directly and unequivocally in conflict with strongly enforced social mores.

Such conflict does not in itself cause irreparable harm, as long as impulses can be acknowledged and given some sanctioned expression, and as long as such thoughts, feelings, and behavior are not covertly stimulated while being overtly forbidden. Thus, for example, life in a monastery may be highly repressive with respect to overt expressions of sex or aggression, but there is no lack of acknowledgment that such impulses exist. Instead, the disciplinary practices of a monastic order are specifically designed to assist its members to confront instinctual drives directly and divert the energy associated with such impulses into services the community defines as useful.

However, complicated problems are created if a community exerts pressure to prevent overt acknowledgement of sexual and aggressive impulses and, at the same time, either covertly stimulates such impulses or establishes conspicuously different standards for children and adults or for men and women. Under such circumstances, impulses that cannot be acknowledged or overtly expressed are likely to gain expression in covert ways—one of which is through the development of hysterical symptoms.

In characterizing an era, social historians rarely have access to actuarial data from which to define a precise central tendency in regard to social customs, values, and personality characteristics. Indeed, the social historian is more concerned with the engagement of the dominant, trend-setting classes in society and with the economic, technological, political, and social forces impinging upon them, for it is this group that gives momentum to cultural change and toward whose standards the more peripheral segments of a society gravitate. Only in this sense the Victorians could be said to have created a family and social climate conducive to the particular mode of conflict resolution Freud identified as "hysterical." The proportion of all western Europeans living in the middle to late nineteenth century in a social-psychological milieu productive of hysterical reactions is, of course, unknown.

It is known that there was a very substantial change in the psychopathology of soldiers between World War I and World War II. The former commonly revealed a variety of hysterical symptoms only infrequently seen a quarter-century later, except among certain subcultures. It is very difficult to find hysterical symptoms in patients in present-day urban centers, unless they were reared in authoritarian households in communities that fully sanctioned such family patterns and were only recently removed from them.

Changes in child-rearing practices and in the pattern of social life are undoubtedly reflected in psychopathology, and changes in the form and nature of emotional disturbance have, in turn, had an effect on the modern practice of psychoanalysis (Rieff 1966).

In present-day society, there is an increasing willingness to acknowledge aggressive impulses and freely satisfy the curiosity children have with respect to sexual matters. Moreover, parental authority and influence have been greatly reduced. Children are freed from tight parental control and family-centered life only to encounter the problems of having to succeed in a number of demanding social circumstances and institutions outside the home. The freedom children and adolescents enjoy has brought with it new responsibility for establishing the values and patterns of behavior that will make up their identity.

Modern parents are uncertain about their mandate to set limits and are, therefore, not well equipped to define accurately what should be approved and what should not. The child or adolescent may be equally in a quandary as to what authority they wish parents to assume, or what behaviors will dependably assure them the love and esteem of adults or peers. The result of this dilemma is the common, present-day syndrome of alienation, aimlessness, anxiety without discernable conflict, and strong feelings of aggression without a well-defined target. Too often the children of today confront parents who are blandly tolerant and understanding but emotionally detached and inconsistant in affection and guidance. If the adolescent or young adult has not had to come to terms with a well-defined and dependable set of parental values and demands, he often feels uncertain of who he is and what he is supposed to do with his life. Consequently he experiences a rather persistent sense of emptiness, lack of direction, and a diffuse anger. Lacking inner direction, he is inclined either to withdraw from any goal-directed activity or to strike out randomly at those institutions of society he believes have failed him.

Psychoanalysis has changed somewhat to accommodate to these new presenting complaints. For one thing, many contemporary analysts have found it desirable at various points in the treatment to engage the patient as a real person rather than serving exclusively as a mirror reflecting feelings and attitudes transferred from parents, siblings, and others. One implication of this is that for many patients the only fully realized and explored relationship they have enjoyed is that with the analyst. Hence the analyst's role extends beyond that of sorting out, through the medium of transference interpretations, the troubled but poignant experiences

emerging from close family ties—the therapist himself becomes an identification figure, perhaps the only person with whom the analysand has
had an authentic, deeply emotional encounter.

Second, psychoanalysts are more concerned with ego processes and
reality testing than with a precise delineation of the vicissitudes of Id
impulses in psychosexual development. In the early history of psychoanalysis comparatively little attention was paid to the patient's management of everyday relationships and problems. It was assumed that these
mundane matters would take care of themselves if the analysis were
successful. Now the manner in which the analysand handles day-to-day
is regarded as appropriate subject matter in analytic sessions.

Third, there is growing propensity to abandon Freud's hardline view
that the limited function of psychoanalysis is to convert the misery of
neurosis into the normal unhappiness of the human condition. Contemporary psychoanalysis intimates that it may have the means of improving
the lot of normally disheartened people rather than merely helping them
to tolerate disappointment and frustration.

THE THERAPEUTIC TECHNIQUE

Over the past thirty years, psychoanalysis has been applied to almost
every facet of life from advertising to art criticism, from politics to economic behavior. Indeed, psychoanalysis has become a theoretical framework for comprehending a very wide range of individual and social
behavior, and in this sense it has become public property rather than the
exclusive province of psychiatrists, psychologists, and social workers.

Such was not the situation in 1882, when Freud, then in his twenties,
first heard of Josef Breuer's hypnotic treatment of a young woman presenting a variety of hysterical symptoms—anesthesia of her right arm
and leg, visual impairment, and loss of capacity to speak her native
language. Four years later, after a period of study with the hypnotist
Charcot in France, Freud set up a medical practice in Vienna in which
he saw many patients with disturbances that were not associated with
any known organic condition and would not yield to conventional medical
treatment. Turning to hypnosis as a tool, he had some successes matching
those of Breuer, but, as the years passed, he became disenchanted with
the technique, since it rarely produced lasting cures and could only
be applied with success to some patients.

By 1896, Freud had adopted a technique of placing patients on a
couch in a quiet room and directing them to report, without reservation,

any thought or feeling that entered their mind. Freud sat out of their line of sight and listened to the stream of consciousness his patients reported. Under these conditions, patients almost invariably expanded on their problems and suggested, sometimes in veiled terms, the nature and source of their neurotic conflicts.

Several important and lasting principles of psychoanalysis were established in these early experiments. First, Freud established the fundamental rule that the patient honestly and unreservedly report everything that comes to mind without questioning its meaning, relevance, importance, or acceptability to the therapist—a very difficult if not impossible task. Second, Freud believed that for free association to be truly free, the patient should be relaxed in a reclining position, the analytic chamber should be quiet and neutrally decorated, and, most important, the analyst should be out of sight. This not only prevented the person of the therapist from being a distraction, but his very invisibility and neutrality tended to evoke fantasies about him on the part of the patient. Fantasies about the therapist, Freud was to learn, often reflected powerful feelings generated in childhood which the patient unconsciously felt toward significant figures in his adult life. Such repressed feelings, brought to consciousness, could be reexamined in the light of the strengths of the adult ego.

PSYCHOANALYTIC PERSONALITY
THEORY

The Structure of Personality

Freud's theory, like most others, is concerned with hypothetical personality structures, with motivation and the transformation of energy, with development, and with an explanation of psychopathology. Freud noted that humans engage in rational, problem-solving behavior as well as in impulsive and sometimes self-destructive behavior, and that they seem to obey various moral and ethical rules even when it is inconvenient to do so. The hypothetical structure designed to mediate between impulse and reality and undertake rational problem-solving he referred to as the *ego*. The structure that contains the basic instinctual drives and is, therefore, the reservoir of psychic energy or *libido* he called the *id*. The structure that incorporates the arbitrary social rules by which conduct is governed, and punishes infractions with guilt, he called the *superego*. It should be clearly understood that these structures do not refer to areas of the brain but are hypothetical constructs invented to help conceptualize how the personality functions. Freud could just as well have called these three aspects of mental life alpha, beta, and gamma functions.

As an additional major structural element, Freud drew a distinction between the *unconscious* and the *conscious*. Between the conscious and the unconscious is a line of demarcation called the *repression barrier*. By definition the id is wholly in the unconscious, the superego largely so, and the ego is partially unavailable to conscious inspection. Again, it must be pointed out that these hypothetical structures have no anatomical analogues; they are simply ways of categorizing mental contents and processes to make sense of observed behavior, including verbal reports of mental life.

Developmental Stages

Infants enter the world with a great deal of diffuse energy but with relatively poor equipment for carrying out any directed activity. Nevertheless, the baby must cope, which means that as quickly as possible he must gain at least a dim understanding of which sources of satisfaction originate within himself and which come from others. This highly important distinction is the first step in ego development and is the basis for subsequent learning. Thus, infants come equipped with the ability to cry. Crying is no great accomplishment, however, until it can be used as a signal to gain attention. At this point the infant has taken an enormously important step. If the neonate's needs for food, warmth, body contact, and movement were perfectly and constantly met, its motivation for learning would be greatly reduced. Or, if it were not cared for when it cried, the signal system would never be learned and it would simply wither away. Thus, at every stage in its development, there must be optimal frustration and satisfaction of the developing child to promote growth and learning.

Freud postulated that the stages of development (the principal developmental tasks) were centered first around satisfying oral needs (at the same time imposing limits on what can be incorporated), next around control of anal sphincters and toilet training (which is much less a need of the infant than one imposed by society), and then on sexuality, culminating in a genital phase in which the young person finally accepts adult responsibilities, becomes dependably heterosexual, and achieves the self-confidence and independence necessary to both.

It is around the issues of gratification versus delay and control versus impulse expression that the socialization of the child is dramatized. If the parent makes a big issue of toilet training and anal control before the infant has the neural equipment to comply, then the infant will attach exceptional importance to the act of withholding or releasing feces, and he will devote a great deal of energy and attention to excremental functions and their symbolic representations. Similarly, if enormous anxiety is generated in the parents by a child's interest in his genitals or his determined competition with the father for the exclusive attention of mother, then the young child may become convinced that his genitals are inordinately powerful and important parts of the self.

If the very young child is not confronted at any stage of development with a demand for performance that is beyond his capacity or understanding, no particular developmental task will become a critical issue for him, and he will be free to devote most of his energy to coping with present problems rather than past conflicts. More concretely, if a child has an optimal, unstressful rearing, he is not given to worrying about whether he will be fed or not, or whether he will defecate or urinate at the right place and at the right time. He learns that he will be fed close to the time he is ready to eat, that his excremental functions are manageable, and that his genitals can be a source of gratification but need not become his sole object in life. Thus, ideally, he is independent, curious about new objects and situations, and has energy available to try to master new challenges.

By contrast, the child traumatized at one or another of the stages of development has to be much more concerned about parental approbation and what must be done to assure it. The parents must be frequently tested and studied, since their positive regard is conditioned and not easily attained. If feeding, excremental functions, or genital play are the focus of energy-consuming real or fantasied transactions with parents, the energy thus consumed is not available for new exploration or adaptation to new problems.

For most of us, the early developmental tasks are solved so that the energy consumed in coping with them is released for service in meeting whatever contemporary issue confronts us. In some instances, however, the resolution is incomplete and the child (or adolescent, or adult) is said to fixate, or have a *fixation* on unsuccessful or only partially successful solutions to a particular development problem. For example, if an adult responds to a wide range of mildly frustrating problems by overeating, he could be said to have an *oral fixation*. The implication is that such an individual never fully solved the problem of oral dependency on the mother and therefore has a propensity to examine every new experience and problem in terms of its implications for either literal or for symbolic feeding. Any failure to achieve or be rewarded by others (if others behave like a bad mother) provokes overeating (being a good mother to one's self).

An individual with a similar but less severe underlying problem might succeed in meeting most problems in a practical, realistic way only to *regress* when exposed to an unusual challenge that might lead to failure. Regression implies retreat from a more advanced form of problem-solving to a more primitive one practiced much earlier in life. Regression can occur at any age, but it is sometimes dramatically revealed in the behavior of a young child when his parents bring a new infant into the household. Well-established toilet training breaks down, dependency increases, and eating problems develop, as the older child tries to be baby again and get the attention most adults shower on infants.

Even moderately severe problems at any of these stages of development are said to lead to the formation of *character traits* that persist throughout life. Thus, oral frustration is thought to appear in the adult disguised as addiction to food or drink or in the form of excessive demands on others for gratification. In the same fashion, problems in the anal stage may be reflected in the adult characteristics of stinginess, stubbornness, and rigidity or in a marked incapacity to manage even ordinary affairs with a degree of orderliness and consistency.

While there is ample clinical evidence that an infancy and childhood fraught with frustration, fear, anxiety, and depreciation make an immutable mark on the adult, it has not been easy to find valid evidence that selective frustrations at various developmental stages indeed produce clearly recognizable adult character types. There are several plausible reasons for this. First, it is unlikely that many parents are exceptionally selective in their responses to the demands of infants at a particular developmental stage. Their attitudes toward and capacities for child-rearing are, rather, likely to be consistently expressed at all stages. Moreover, since the stages themselves are not sharply demarcated, it would be difficult even if desired to focus exclusively on the behaviors, feelings, or emotions associated with a single developmental sequence. Finally, while certain rather fundamental personality characteristics may well be established very early in life, there remains, even in emotionally handicapped people, a substantial reserve capacity for coping with the demands of life. All individuals are pulled or pushed toward solutions to problems and standards of behavior that are acceptable to their particular social group. Sometimes these adaptations are only fragile and superficial. More frequently, however, the gratifications of socially endorsed forms of behavior greatly reduce the attractiveness of deviant behavior.

It is theoretically, if not practically, possible for an individual to be reared with an optimal kind and quality of frustration and satisfaction that would ensure a maximum of ego development and a minimum of repression. In Freudian terms, this person would convert most of his instinctual energy into seeking the gratifications of work and love that produce only a tolerable amount of social censure and restriction.

Repression and Neurosis

In fact, even the most loving and intelligent of parents cannot provide optimal rearing for their children, principally because social prescriptions for behavior only rarely conform to the needs of the individual child. What the child is supposed to be able to do at a given age almost never coincides with what he is, in fact, able, willing, or ready to do. Even the best of parents cannot escape being too frustrating or too indulgent at times. When a child is severely frustrated, he cannot learn, and when he is over indulged, he has no need to. The frustrated child cannot test reality because he anxiously avoids open confrontations; the overindulged child cannot test reality because no well-defined external boundaries have ever been imposed, and the only reality is his impulse of the moment.

All of us are neurotic to one degree or another in that we overinterpret, underinterpret, or misinterpret reality according to our childhood experiences. As noted earlier, the infant enters the world with a blossoming complement of instinctual drives and is entrapped by adults waiting to shape him into a civilized product. The infant lacks the capacity to sort things out and get them in some sort of perspective. And, if the young child is confronted with problems far beyond his capacity to resolve or comprehend, his limited resources permit him only to push the problem outside the range of events with which he will concern himself. That is, he will *repress* those elements of a problem that cannot be handled.

We do not know exactly how repression occurs. It appears that when a young child has strongly conflictual experiences, the less workable of the two is repressed. For example, if a mother sometimes engages in rather hateful, punitive behavior toward a young child and at other times is affectionate and playful, the child has two real but incompatible images of mother. It is clearly functional for the child to erase the frightening view of mother, along with any associated thoughts or feelings. The child quite naturally attempts to help keep the image of a good mother in consciousness as much of the time as possible.

If, however, the mother is irritable, angry, and punitive most of the time and only occasionally really affectionate, it may be functional for the child to repress any image of a tender mother, since a tender mother would be conducive to his relaxing his guard. Under these circumstances the child (and later the adult) will experience anxiety in the face of warm, loving gestures from others, unlike most individuals who have repressed the bad-mother image and are therefore made anxious by punitive, controlling behavior. H. S. Sullivan (1947) most clearly enunciated this position, a conception that is compatible with contemporary views.

A repressed thought or feeling is in one sense out of mind. Yet it continues to exist and is incapable of modification by subsequent experience. For example, a mother might have great anxieties about caring for a very young child but become considerably more relaxed as the child grows older. If the child has an image of a desperate, anxious mother which is repressed when he is very young, the image cannot be fully corrected by more up-to-date observations. It remains alive in the unconscious and is a potentially complicating factor in his later relationships with his mother and indeed with all women.

We now have a picture of personality in which a great deal of potentially explosive psychic content may have been sealed off from expression in consciousness and, as a consequence, gone unmodified by corrective experience. Such exaggerated and primitive expressions of libidinal drives as smearing, soiling, biting, stabbing, killing, or perverse expressions of sexual impulses were, presumably, greeted with strong disapprobation early in life and quickly repressed. If the unconscious could speak, it might say something like, "If I am aggressive, sexually assertive, competitive, or demanding to mommy (or all women like mommy) or daddy (or all men or men like daddy), they will hate, destroy, take advantage of, abandon, or punish me." As a corollary it could also be stated: "If I am obedient, polite, submissive, self-abnegating, and passive in relations with mother or father they (all women or all men) will love, cherish, support, and admire me." Either of these exaggerated, emotionally toned sets of beliefs will complicate life for a child, adolescent, or adult.

Adults are of course presumptuous in assuming that they have accurate insight into what goes on in an infant's psyche. Obviously, no infant or young child can communicate just what is going on in his mind. Thus, the attributions made to the young child are partly metaphorical statements, partly inferences drawn from close observation of the behavior of very young children, and partly reconstructions made on the basis of adult memories of childhood.

In touch with the world, people, and with this personal prison camp of anxiety-provoking impulses, wishes, and ideas is the ego. Again, speaking metaphorically, if the ego is big, strong, and flexible and the prisoners behind the repression barrier are relatively few in number (either because some have been neutralized and allowed conscious expression or because most infantile impulses were received calmly by parents and openly evaluated in reality terms), there is no problem. On the other hand, if the ego is small, weak, and rigid (because it has had too many problems to solve too soon) and the prisoners are big, tough, and tricky, there is substantial difficulty. The weak ego must expend a large part of its resources in keeping the repression barrier intact and is forever involved in anxiety-ridden exercises to keep the prisoners under control.

The repression barrier is like a fence in a concentration camp. It is difficult for the prisoners to escape, but if they are aroused by some situation outside the camp they will make an extra effort to slip through the wire, overpower the ego, and force it into activity that is "wrong," unrealistic, or both. One repressed self-image that almost everyone has (because everyone was once a small child and frequently failed to meet life's challenges) is that of impotent dependence. If, as an adolescent or young adult, one faces a difficult but important examination, this particular repressed self-image may be agitated and try to gain access to the ego. If this is successful, the ego may try to avoid the examination (regress) and seek the doubtful comfort of escape to a less demanding mode of life. Or the ego may resist the impulse to do this because it is clearly more realistic to face up to the examination. But the efforts of the self-image of impotent-dependency to escape through the repression barrier may thwart this rational plan by utilizing the weapon of *anxiety*. The ego may attempt to deny anxiety. It may *rationalize* that this agitation is due to too much coffee or lack of sleep the night before, or it may conjure up other reasons for it. In psychoanalytic terms, any or all of these energy-consuming mental activities are designed by the ego to prevent impulsive flight from the difficult confrontation at the cost of lowered efficiency. It is the person who is frequently anxious, and who devotes more time to defensive evasions than to productive work, who seeks psychoanalysis.

THE TOOLS OF THERAPY

Probably most patients who seek out a psychoanalyst are simply aware of hurting in ways sometimes difficult to articulate accurately. Some may feel emotionally subdued, detached, unfulfilled, and incapable of seeking vigorously and zestfully the gratifications in life that people around them seem to find. Others may feel out of control in the sense of being emotionally labile, incapable of making lasting commitments, and conscious of endless running without a clear objective. Both categories of clients probably feel disappointed and guilty about failures in relationships with others, and both may have transient or chronic psychogenic ailments.

The developmental theory outlined above holds that the felt lack of gratification, lack of competence, lack of self-control, and lack of physical well-being are indications that a significant part of the ego's energy is directed not toward the engagement of reality in the interests of maximizing socially condoned impulse expression but toward the management of anxiety generated by the prisoners locked behind the repression barrier. In soliciting the analyst's help, the patient, more often than not, is seeking relief but not basic change. The analysand hopes the treatment will greatly enhance his capacities for finding gratification without uncovering the source of the unproductive drain on the ego's energies. He usually does not seek the release and rehabilitation of the prisoners behind the repression barrier, but a more efficient control system that will relieve him of the need to endlessly patrol the barrier.

While the analyst may initially seem to be allied with the ego in keeping the lid on the unconscious, in fact he intends to induce the patient to open the gates and let out the prisoners. That is, he anticipates that he can help his patient look squarely and unflinchingly at the repressed aspects of his experience, rehabilitate the prisoners, and put them to work for the ego in coping with reality problems.

Transference

The analyst accomplishes his goals with the aid of the therapeutic tool of *transference*. In its original meaning, transference referred to the crossing of the repression barrier by repressed wishes or thoughts—in some disguise, naturally, like spies from an enemy army. Dreams, for example, are thought to be one means by which forbidden impulses are transferred across the barrier. More recently, the term transference has come to be used mainly to refer to irrational attachments to or beliefs about others. These beliefs or feelings may be plausible, but they are irrational in that they are not based on evidence or are based on flimsy evidence. If the boss asks you, a hard-working employee, to drop in to see him, and you break out in a cold sweat and anticipate being fired, that is transference. If, on short acquaintance, you fall madly in love with a girl who you believe will make your life a paradise on earth, that is transference.

This characterization of transference is more neo-Freudian than classical. In Freud's original formulation, the definition of transference was limited to intense feelings of the analysand toward the analyst—feelings that were originally directed to the analysand's parents. Freud was convinced that the patient actually hallucinated the image of the parent in the special atmosphere of the analyst's chamber. According to this view, the analyst is not judged by the patient to be like his parent but actually *is* the parent. The analyst is merely a mirror, or blank screen, on which the analysand projects vividly the emotional turmoil of his developmental history.

The *transference neurosis* is forged out of this intense reenactment of psychological trauma. That is, the entire drama of psychosexual development is replayed, this time with the analyst as the target of sexual and aggressive impulses, cast in the roles of both parents (in periods of mother transference or father transference, depending on the particular developmental issue under scrutiny). In this reenactment, the drama of phychosexual development need not end the same way, since the analyst is detached, nonjudgmental, and essentially passive, except for his efforts at interpretation. Through the agency of interpretation, previously unconscious feelings and beliefs are brought under conscious scrutiny, and the transference neurosis is ultimately dissolved. The analysand is thus presumed to be freed of his neurotic conflicts.

However, in the course of the analysis, while the analyst is equated in the patient's unconscious with parental figures, he is seen as a dispenser of rewards and punishments. Thus, the patient may lose symptoms and in other ways appear healthier because he expects to be rewarded or to avoid punishment. Such favorable changes are called *transference improvements* or, if dramatic in their extent, *transference cures*.

Contemporary psychoanalysis is moving away from the concept of the analyst as a mirror. It is now conjectured that even when silent and out of sight, the analyst inevitably communicates to his patient, through shifts in position, changes in breathing, the scratch of his pen, and so on. Since these nonverbal behaviors occur in an atmosphere of relative stimulus deprivation, they can become very consequential to the analysand. To the analysand, a change in the analyst's position may reflect approval or disapproval of a particular associational sequence, interest or boredom, or some other change in attitude that could be of great importance. More attention is now being paid to the real relationship between the analyst and the analysand, and to how it is differentiated from the transference relationship. To the extent that the real analyst participates in the relationship, the possibility of the analysand's projecting a hallucinated parent figure on the analyst seems much reduced.

Perhaps we should be content in saying that whenever arbitrary, emotionally charged beliefs generated in early childhood about a mother (and, by extension, women in general), a father (or men in general), or siblings (peers in general) are evoked by contemporary persons, including the therapist (without his having done anything to provoke these responses), this can be thought of as a transference phenomenon. The word has been badly misused by being extended to any and all kinds of emotional pain or pleasure in a relationship, but the phenomenon is best understood when restricted to those intense feelings one person has about another that have no realistic basis. This is not to say that there are no transference elements in normal relationships, or that there are no reality elements in sudden, inexplicable attachments to or rejections of others. These elements exist, of course, but they usually create no particular difficulty in our everyday relationships.

The analyst uses the transferences of the patient to help him. The patient relives his troubled life in the secure relationship with the analyst and comes to see that unpleasant complications in his life derive from his having applied distorted beliefs, values, and feelings, and inappropriate coping devices generated in childhood to contemporary relationships and situations. By working through in painful detail in his relationship with his analyst all the unrealistic, anxiety-evoking feelings and beliefs about self and others learned in the course of growing up, the analysand is presumed to be freed to reassess his contemporary relationships and put them on a more realistic basis.

Needless to say, this aim cannot be realized if the analyst reacts in such a way as to reconfirm the very distortions of which the patient hopes to be relieved. If the therapist is made so anxious by the patient's symptoms that he reacts with anger, aloofness, or seductive friendliness, he can scarcely assist the analysand to work through his problems. Ideally, the analyst is a decent, tolerant, patient, thoughtful person who, through his personal analysis and his analytic training, has dissolved the more troublesome of his own transference feelings. That is, an analyst ought to have relatively few counter-transference reactions to his patients; he should not become overly attached to patients or irritated by them because they stir up unresolved conflicts in him. This does not preclude the analyst's liking his patients because of qualities they possess, nor does it rule out the analyst's disliking some things his patients do. But the analyst should not become angry or anxious when confronted by his patient with accusations or characterizations that emerge from the analysand's recapitulation of his traumatic history.

Resistance

When a patient seeks psychotherapy, he is pretty well convinced that his life is troubled. However, he may also be convinced that not he, but others with whom he is associated, are the source of that trouble. Moreover, while his adjustment may be faulty, it may still be the best adjustment he has ever managed, and the prospect of a new approach to life might seem even more painful. Finally, while he may recognize that his solutions to problems of living are faulty, he may retain a powerful attachment to some of them.

Thus, the ambivalent analysand may *resist* accepting responsibility for his own acts; he may *resist* trying new solutions; and he may *resist* giving up traits and coping devices he admires, even if almost no one around him does. An even greater resistance must eventually be dissolved in the course of analysis—resistance to opening the gates of the unconscious and letting out all the feared prisoners. All other forms of resistance are byproducts of the patient's fears of what he would discover in his unconscious if these gates were opened. For this reason, the analysand cannot conceive that the therapist really wants him to engage in what seems to him such an unwholesome enterprise. Analysands, like the rest of us, want to improve their capabilities to meet problems of living without actually disturbing the source of their incapacities.

Defenses

A *defense,* in the psychological sense of the term, is a largely unconscious stratagem by which an individual attempts to reveal no more of the truth about himself to himself or to others than he finds convenient and tolerable. *Amnesia* (the literal forgetting of traumatic events), *repression,* (a kind of forgetting that has already been discussed), and *suppression* (a willful, selective inattention to significant data) are the more primitive and comprehensive defenses. Defenses are effective to the extent that one cannot be held responsible for or be anxious about aspects of self that do not seem to exist. But they are ineffective in that these aspects of self do in fact exist, even if they are forgotten, and they make it difficult for the ego to achieve stable, reasonable, and realistic solutions to the complex problems of living. Hence, another class of defenses must be brought into play to repair logical gaps created by unconscious id or superego impulses that are pushing in one direction while reality pulls in another.

An anxiety-provoking impulse may be gotten rid of through a process of *projection*—by attributing the impulse to another person or category of people. Intensely lustful feelings about another woman's husband, for example, might provoke intense shame and guilt in a woman whose conscience harshly forbids such feelings. Or such lustful feelings might create intense anxiety if they were constant, seemed on the verge of going out of control, and could lead to an abrupt loss of self-esteem if expressed. However, if the lust were perceived as that of the other person, it would be easier to cope with—it would be *his* problem, not hers. It is thus a convenient fiction to attribute frightening and unacceptable impulses to others, since one's consciousness may still be filled with thoughts of lust, but free of shame or guilt. It would seem natural to be concerned about the fact that a friend's husband was so taken with one's charms that his every action betrayed his sordid intentions.

Phobic reactions can achieve a similar defensive outcome. If a woman has a guilt-producing impulse to make sexual advances to the husband of her best friend, an effective means of controlling the impulse while punishing herself is a growing fear of leaving her house. Any forbidden impulse can be linked with a place, an object, or a particular situation and thereby externalized. It is easier to be afraid of cats, high places, open fields, closets, or whatever, that can be avoided than something within oneself that cannot.

In its acute form, a phobic reaction may be quite dramatic and disabling; in a milder form, it may amount to no more than a strong disinclination to put oneself in certain physical or social situations even when it would be advantageous to do so. For example, many people have a well-developed fear of the dark, of riding in airplanes, or of speaking or performing in public. Since these are not inherently dangerous activities, and since they are sometimes necessary, it is always interesting to conjecture what dangerous inner impulses are being converted into fears of these situations.

Reaction formation, a defensive device which is dramatic in its extreme form (an example is the vigorous opponent of pornography who spends most of his life examining obscene books, photographs, and movies in order to carry out his crusade against them), appears in a more subdued form in the psychic repertoire of most people. Many individuals, when troubled over a forbidden impulse, express the precise opposite of the urge they wish to deny. A person who is disorganized and anxious because of sexual feelings may adopt a highly rigorous and restrictive moral code which severely limits contact with anything remotely suggestive of sex. A person who copes poorly with intense, diffuse anger may become intensely opposed to violence. Indeed, given the complexity of life and the difficulty of finding simple answers to most personal or social problems, one may suspect an unconscious motive at the basis of any passionately advocated, uncomplicated, comprehensive solution to a problem.

Solutions to early childhood problems which have been repressed tend to be both comprehensive and impractical. When these comprehensive solutions emerge in the adult mind, they are rationalized in order to make them plausible. For example, a very young child may entertain the convenient fantasy of eliminating all his siblings in order to solve the problem of competition for his parents' love and attention. Since his primitive superego suggests that he might be killed for having such thoughts (his siblings might have identical thoughts, or grownups might punish him for having them), the solution is repressed. If later in life (as often occurs in early adolescence) there is a recurrence of intense competition with peers for limited quantities of approbation and attention, the early repressed solution may reappear. However, since the solution "kill all competitors" cannot be allowed access to consciousness without producing shame and anxiety, the thought that emerges may be, "The way to solve human problems is for people to love one another!" If one loves everyone, he cannot compete with them, since this would be aggressive. The obvious solution is to withdraw from any activity in which there is the possibility of competition and devote full time to loving. Freed from the competitive urge by this psychic maneuver, the full-time lover of all mankind feels temporarily at peace with himself. However, the original, unconscious, hostile competitive drive is not extinguished and may, finding one outlet for expression blocked, seek another. Aggressive drives may be turned against the self. Although this is a hypothetical example, it may have some application to the many alienated adolescents who, seeking love in a hippie community, manage to find only a kind of social self-destruction in disease, malnutrition, poverty, and drug abuse.

Some defenses operate in a more conscious mode—the defender has a greater awareness of what is taking place. For example, if out of motives he does not understand, one does something unreasonable or unrealistic, he may *rationalize* by devising an explanation others will accept as plausible. One may also *intellectualize* (convert inconvenient and anxiety-evoking impulses into elaborate verbal exercises), or *displace* impulses (direct impulses at targets other than those for which they are really intended).

The catalogue of deceits humans practice to disown repressed impulses and fears is exceptionally large, and these defensive maneuvers are often very difficult to discern. This problem is especially complicated by the fact that a substantial proportion of a patient's visible behavior does not change at all as a consequence of analysis. The only change may be in the attitude or emotional tone with which familiar activities are carried out, or an increase in the level of conscious scrutiny of one's activities. That is, what was once done because the patient had no alternative is now undertaken consciously in conformity with reality principles.

A researcher would have a difficult time measuring the effectiveness of psychoanalysis. Once the more obtrusive symptoms and transparent defensive maneuvers have disappeared and there are indications of satisfactory adjustment in major areas of living, a question arises as to what is left to be recorded.

THE THERAPEUTIC PROCESS

Both the analyst and the successful analysand would surely say that most therapeutic changes, while subtle and perhaps impossible to measure reliably, are, nevertheless, subjectively very important. Among these significant changes is an ability to live with anxiety long enough to examine its probable source—a capacity to look at one's own behavior and to stop deceiving oneself. Related to this is a willingness to undertake some genuine tests of reality and to accept with a degree of stoicism both the successes and failures that are inevitable if one fully engages life.

The full results of a successful analysis that has as its objective, "where id was, there shall ego be," can only be suggested. Analysis is not a glorified Dale Carnegie course in which all the solutions to life's problems are suddenly made clear. It is not training in a superior etiquette that makes all relationships smooth and untroubled. It may even make life harder in many respects, since the successful analysand can no longer gloss over the realistically difficult problems, retreat from them, or defend himself against facing them. It offers a life that lacks magical solutions but permits realistic if unglamorous ones. In the well-analyzed person's life, other people are seen neither as benevolent magicians or as ogres but as fully three-dimensional human beings.

It is this elimination of high drama in life that many analysands resist, even though the drama has produced more pain than pleasure. It is difficult for many individuals to contemplate realistic, anxiety-free accomplishment in work, or an unencumbered uncomplicated love relationship, because, never having had such experiences, they seem rather drab. Nevertheless, this is all analysis offers.

Since everyone suffers frustration, and since experiences conflict to some degree in the course of psychosexual development, it follows that psychoanalysis should benefit anyone capable of undertaking it. One does not need disabling symptoms to qualify for psychoanalysis, and many analysts would even assert that analysis is an experimental procedure for studying depth psychology rather than a method of treatment. Nevertheless, most applicants for analysis are burdened with an array of problems, and it is here that treatment begins.

Positive Transference

In theory, treatment is an orderly procedure. Initially there is a positive transference, born of the patient's faith that the analyst, like the all-powerful mother or father, has the capacity to relieve him promptly of his psychic pain. The positive aspects of the relationship are strengthened by the observation that the analyst is nonjudgmental and neutrally accepting of whatever the patient says or does. Sometimes this unprecedented experience of threat-free and criticism-free contact is so refreshing that the patient immediately feels elated and improved and is said to have achieved a transference cure. Some leave analysis at this point, believing they have accomplished their purpose, but those who accept the analyst's interpretation that this sense of well-being is a transference phenomenon push on to grapple with the basic problems that have yet to appear.

Following the basic rule of verbalizing all associations as they enter the mind, the patient scans his life experiences, usually moving back and forth between the present and the past. As he does so, he encounters a wide array of half-truths; instances of stubborn categorical judgments; painful memories of seeming injustice, deceit, and punitiveness on the part of himself and others; countless examples of distortion, ambiguity, and misplaced emphasis; and finally a painful revivification of childhood emotions he believed extinct.

In this welter of material, the patient, with the help of the analyst, learns about his defenses—the set of deceptions he uses to keep intact comfortable fictions about himself and others. As these defenses are dissolved the patient may feel empty, exposed, and anxious, for he learns the nature of the prisoners locked behind the repression barrier and fears what might happen if the gates to the unconscious were fully opened.

Negative Transference

His apprehensions are first triggered by the increasing frequency with which irrational, emotionally toned, and anxiety-evoking thoughts about the analyst and others in his life make their appearance. At this point, he begins to feel that the analyst is not helping him but making him worse. Put another way, the analyst, at first greeted as a powerful ally, now seems to be a traitor who is really on the side of the rebellious prisoners. The analyst is now reacted to as if he were the parents who, in the patient's childhood, had the power to hurt, frustrate, and demean him, and the analysis enters a period of negative transference during which resistance becomes more evident. Resistance can take many forms—long periods of silence, endless circumlocutions, relating of irrelevant anecdotes, obsessive preoccupation with some minor current or past events, missed analytic hours, lateness to appointments, and so on. When these maneuvers are interpreted as resistances to facing primary problems, the patient feels backed up against a wall. Moreover, the analyst is often seen as incompetent, overbearing, and unhelpful. Just as some patients escape from analysis while basking in the glow of positive transference, others leave during the period of negative transference, when they begin to feel more anxious and less well adjusted than before treatment.

While the patient is suffering increasingly intense anxiety and dysphoria, what is the analyst doing? From the viewpoint of most patients, he rarely does anything, and certainly not as much as the patient would hope. The classical analyst would see his primary responsibility as that of remaining a blank screen, of intervening only infrequently, to interpret either resistance or transference. While such behavior may be frustrating and even infuriating to the analysand, who is exerting all efforts to engage the analyst as a person, it is essential if the patient is finally to accept completely the notion that he and no one else controls his destiny.

The patient's objective is to prove that his parents (or derivative contemporary associates) and then the analyst have the key to a state of well-being and must be induced to hand it over. The analyst, on the other hand, takes the position that only the patient has the key, and he must be induced to find it.

The analysand gets through periods of positive and negative transference because he remains convinced that the analyst has the gift of happiness to give. Meanwhile the analyst remains—if one can imagine such a thing—a friendly rock. The patient cajoles, threatens, pleads, seduces, and offers bribes or insults in order to make the analyst give him happiness, or expiation. All the analyst can do is patiently stand by while the analysand exhausts his stock of deceits and ploys designed to get others to give him a gratifying life and begins to examine his own resources for gaining pleasure from loving and working. Many contemporary analysts are departing from this approach on the grounds that absolute frustration of the analysand's wish to be fed is not as productive as a more balanced diet in which real, contemporary relating, which may involve a certain amount of attention to the patient's reality problem, is interspersed with periods in which transference material is prominent.

The classical analyst regards such departures as rather deceitful on the grounds that he really has no magic to dispense. The new breed of psychoanalytic therapist, however, is equally convinced that a judicious catering to the patient's dependency needs considerably enhances the realistic, problem-solving approach of the therapeutic engagement. They argue that the strict classical approach is so foreign from any shared human experience that it cannot be helpful to most patients.

What keeps analysands in the therapeutic relationship during low periods varies. Sometimes it is a helpless, frustrated dependency; sometimes it is simply a character trait that demands that all jobs be finished, regardless of how pleasant or unpleasant; and sometimes the prime mover is pressure from others with whom the patient is intimate. Of course, what should keep the analysis underway is the patient's increasing capacity to distinguish between transference projections and a realistic awareness of the analyst's steady, neutral interest and willingness to help the patient find his own solutions.

Working Through

Once the period of negative transference is successfully negotiated, the patient is likely to begin persistently replaying the dramatic events of early childhood, with the analyst cast in the role of the parents or siblings. The patient develops the same intense feelings of anger, impotence, dependency, jealousy, envy, and so on that he experienced as a young child, but this time it is in the company of a friendly, neutral, supportive, nonthreatening person. The resolution of this transference neurosis is the key to change in the patient. In effect, the analysand is given a second chance to form beliefs and feelings about himself and others. The prisoners behind the repression barrier are released one by one and are seen to be life sized rather than terrifying monsters. One by one, the threatening impulses and fears are reexamined, and realistic decisions can be made about how they can be reconciled with the patient's current life. The patient is able to perceive that he is now an adult among adults and is therefore capable of either independent or fully collaborative striving toward goals of his own choosing. He can make a candid assessment of his abilities and relate them to what is realistically achievable. He can be normally aggressive without being sadistic; he can show affection without fear either of being swallowed up in a helpless dependency or of having to control the loved one; he can succeed without fear that others will be made angry; and he can fail without fearing ridicule. In summary, he can treat his impulses as rather friendly beasts that can be properly trained to enrich his life with their spontaneity but also to keep off the furniture and not bite visitors.

Clearly this procedure, while easy to describe, is often very protracted and full of pitfalls in actual practice. Relatively early in an analysis there may be a substantially complete disclosure and accurate identification of core conflicts and significant thematic material, but it remains for these distortions to be exemplified in the transference neurosis and then painstakingly *worked through*. A neurotic distortion may be expressed in many ways in the context of the transference, and each manifestation must be noted and patiently analyzed.

Eventually, when all the deceits and misperceptions that comprise the neurosis have been thoroughly worked through, the transference is also dissolved, and the analyst is seen realistically as one healthy adult sees another. A terminal phase in contemporary analyses may then be a working through in another sense. The analysand may test out his newly gained maturity of outlook and freedom to engage and by examining outcomes with the analyst on a reality basis.

The successful analysand, as mentioned earlier, is presumed to be able to control instinctual drives in the interests of his own gratification rather than being driven by them. However, Freud himself was not as encouraging in his description of the possible outcomes of analysis as this view may suggest. He never took the position that psychoanalysis resolved all or even most of life's problems. Indeed, he was somewhat pessimistic about the utility of the technique in treating any but a relatively narrow range of emotional disturbances—the so-called transference neuroses, including hysteria, anxiety states, phobias and obsessive-compulsive disorders. Freud never aspired to do more than replace the misery created by neurotic symptoms with the commonplace unhappiness of humans in a hard world.

Moreover, the orderly theoretical sequence of events in analysis, outlined above, is not often seen in reality. Both patient and analyst are caught up in a task that has no clear guidelines for successful completion. The stages are not clear cut, and apparent progress may be wiped out at any time by the disclosure of profound conflicts and fears previously unsuspected. The analysand may be detained for months on certain issues that seem to require clarification before further progress can be made. Moreover, analysts, however well trained and personally well analyzed, retain blind spots and resistances to understanding what the patient is trying to communicate. Both patient and therapist must often struggle hard to separate reality from transference distortions.

On top of all this, there is a wide range of techniques practiced under the title psychoanalysis, and there are idiosyncrasies of individual analysts that cannot be excluded from the analytic relationship. In the end, one is left with the conclusion that any therapy that conscientiously takes transference and resistance into account as the core of the treatment must be viewed as psychoanalytic. Such an assertion is likely to evoke clamorous dissent from the several schools of psychoanalysis that have institutionalized training programs and firmly identify as psychoanalysis what their graduates practice in transactions with their patients. What graduates do, however, seems to fall over as wide a range as their explanations for adopting the particular practices they use.

A CASE THERAPY

Let us imagine that Ginny, the daughter of Grace H. in *The Quiet Furies* (McNeil, 1967), has undertaken analysis. Ginny actually sought, and made excellent use of, brief psychotherapy at a time of crisis in her life. In the course of her therapy, she not only obtained the support necessary to enable her to marry and separate from her hypochondriacal and domineering mother, but she also obtained some insight into her identification with her mother—her own propensity to resolve problems by becoming ill.

We do not have a detailed history of Ginny's life and must therefore make many conjectures, but we do know that she would be regarded as a prime candidate for psychoanalysis. At age twenty-six she had had serious difficulty in establishing her independence from her mother and in contemplating marriage in opposition to her mother's wishes. Nevertheless, she had functioned well most of her life, had graduated from college, and had worked productively without undue anxiety.

At first glance, one might be inclined to say that all of Ginny's problems were created by her mother, and that if her mother changed, Ginny could change. However, while her mother represented a disagreeable reality, Ginny was not only not meeting her mother's maneuvers on a realistic basis, but was covertly using her mother to resolve her own ambivalent feelings about marriage. Thus, there was much that Ginny could change in herself to enhance the probability of her meeting her current and future problems more effectively.

In the opening hours, before the analysis is formally begun, the analyst obtains a case history, explains the fundamental rule, works out a plan for payment of fees, and deals with any other problems, such as appointment times. With the begining of the analysis, the analyst situates himself out of sight behind the couch on which Ginny is reposing and waits for her to speak.

Tentatively at first, and then with feeling, Ginny expresses her anger about her mother, vividly recounting the ways in which she has made life in their family difficult. The pleasant, neutral analyst gives largely silent assent to Ginny's diatribe, in sharp contrast to her mother who argues vigorously if she is opposed or criticized. Thus Ginny begins to feel very attached to the analyst, in whom, if he is a male, she finds some of the good characteristics of her father greatly enlarged and without the negative features. Moreover, she feels very well, having unburdened herself, and more competent to face problems than ever before. She somewhat shyly confides her affection for the analyst and alludes to his great skills in helping her to achieve remarkable improvements in so short a time. She may suggest termination on the grounds that she has gained what she came for and would not profit from further sessions.

At this juncture the analyst's tactics may include appropriately timed observations that Ginny has not commented at any length about herself and her own problems, that her reports of her handling of difficult situations suggest that she may identify with her mother's hypochondriasis, since she also develops physical symptoms in periods of crisis, that she handles some aspects of her relationship with her mother in such a way as to evoke the very behavior she claims to fear and resent, and so on. In this way the analyst suggests that their work has really just begun, that Ginny's good feelings are in part the product of her not really looking at herself closely, and that there are, quite possibly, some complicated truths about her relationship with her family that remained to be uncovered. Since Ginny in one sense already knows that there are undisclosed and conflictual elements in her feelings toward significant people in her life, and also knows that examination of these elements would be painful and anxiety-provoking, she is not eager to pursue them. Moreover, she has given the analyst a rare gift of trust, approbation, and even affection, and he seems to spurn her.

What can we reasonably conjecture about the prisoners Ginny holds in repression? Some, such as a far-reaching dependency-independency conflict, are shared with most people, simply by virtue of having once been weak and small and necessarily dependent. In the same category would be wildly unrealistic, comprehensive solutions to conflicts associated with early psychosexual development—fantasies of total control of significant others or of completely unbounded impulse expression. More specific to Ginny's history, one can infer an inordinate fear as a young child that she had the capacity to kill her hypochondriacal mother, coupled with some relish apparently at possessing the power to do so. We may also conjecture that her surface antagonism to her mother is matched by hidden admiration for the strength reflected in her mother's capacity to terrorize the household. We can guess that as a girl she had a deep attachment to her father, competing with intense anger at the impotence that made him incapable of protecting her. We note Ginny's ambivalence with respect to marriage, which may be linked to the equation, disobedience equals mother's death, but could also be tied to profound unconscious fears of loss of dependency. She, like her mother, might have to be dominant because men are weak. But domination requires independence and threatens potential loss of love.

The analyst's gentle nudging toward exploration of these highly emotion-laden unconscious conflicts leaves Ginny feeling depressed, angry, and anxious. She now perceives the analyst as rejecting, unhelpful, and incompetent. Again, she thinks of terminating the relationship, now so painful.

In the next phase, the rather diffuse feelings of antagonism toward the analyst begin to coalesce around particular issues. For long periods she inveighs angrily against the analyst's impotence (like her father's) and then is equally upset at his controlling, dominating, critical behavior (like her mother's). As Ginny replays these poignant episodes from her childhood, the analyst remains his professionally decent, discerning, neutral self and, as the occasion seems to demand, interprets the transference. In effect, Ginny has the experience of reliving the traumatic events of her life, but with a different outcome. Instead of evoking real or imagined anger, rejection, abject dependency, or lonely independence, her fantasies and emotions evoke only warm support to examine them in the light of her adult capabilities for understanding.

As Ginny works through the release of one imprisoned fear, conflict, or fantasy after another, she can see that they do not place her in the desperate jeopardy she feared in childhood, but are simply distortions that can now be corrected. At the conclusion of analysis, Ginny will still have to cope with her mother, the responsibilities of marriage, and personal ambitions. All of these will be realistically difficult to handle, and there will be much unhappiness as well as gratification in the process. But Ginny will be free of intense, disabling anxiety and ambivalence in the face of realistic problems and the tendency to respond impulsively and erratically when decisions must be made. She will have a realistic view of her own capacities, and will see herself neither as a malevolent force nor as an omnipotent, saving angel.

To reach these outcomes Ginny will have devoted anywhere from $10,000 to $30,000 and from 500 to 2000 hours of her time, extending over a period of a year to four or five years. Whether approximately similar results could have been obtained in a shorter period with correspondingly less expense is a question the reader can try to decide for himself in reading the following chapters.

Behavior Therapy

Behavior therapists are confronted with the same sets of clinical data available to psychosocial conflict theorists and fulfillment theorists. They too wish to understand human behavior and be helpful to individuals with problems. There is substantial agreement among theorists about the range of problems patients bring to therapists, but there is substantial disagreement about the origins of reported symptoms and the means by which they can be eliminated or reduced in severity.

LEARNING THEORY

Basic Drives

All theorists, including behaviorists, start with suppositions, but behaviorists suppose rather different things than Freudians or Rogerians. First of all they suppose—not unlike Freudians—that there are certain biological drives with which we are all endowed. The list varies, but sex, hunger, thirst, and body contact are frequently included. These comprise the so-called deficit motivations: the organism is stirred to action if it is hungry, thirsty, sexually aroused, or isolated from its kind. In humans, as in other vertebrates, these genetically determined motivations, with related skills and physical equipment, are released under favorable environmental conditions. The conditions are so minimal, except for sex, that almost no one fails to develop the capability of satisfying these

112

needs, given the availability of suitable supplies in the environment. However, humans along with many other organisms, appear to also have built-in propensities for aggression or dominance and exploration or curiosity. It is clearly not enough for an organism merely to learn how to eat and drink and perform the sexual act or associate with other members of its species. If food, water, an appropriate sexual object, or other members of the species are not readily available, the organism must have some elementary capability for searching them out and over-coming obstacles to need-satisfaction. For a long time it was assumed that aggression and curiosity were simply part of the apparatus for deficit need-satisfaction and were automatically turned off when thirst was slaked, hunger allayed, or lust satisfied. More recently, observers have permitted themselves to see that animals, even those with rather low rankings on the phylogenetic scale, continue to explore their environment even when they are well fed, water filled, and sexually satiated. Indeed, it became evident that in the primates merely entertaining activities are often placed ahead of eating, drinking, and sex. Since it is obvious in humans and easily noted in animals that motivation is not extinguished by satiation of physical needs, it is difficult now to understand how anyone could ever have seriously concluded that all human behavior had its roots in deficit motivation.

The human infant, child, adolescent, and adult more or less constantly manipulate their social and physical environment, not because such engagements are essential to survival, but because exercise of complex skills is intrinsically satisfying. This human capacity for self-stimulation and constant reformulation of experience through the medium of language is somewhat troublesome for the strict behaviorist. He asks us to believe that from a developmental standpoint all motivation is derivative from physiological needs through a process of *secondary reinforcement*. Thus, if the behaviorist could exert total control over the conditions under which physiological needs are met, he could control all behavior of the organism. If aggression and exploration are seen as existing solely in the interests of satisfying such needs, then these behaviors could also be brought under control.

On the other hand, if aggression and exploration are seen as powerful built-in potentialities in their own right, rather than as derivative from physiological deficits, the problem of control becomes more complex. If one adds the apparent capacity of humans to transpose and transform experience and to behave in ways not predictable from the environmental input, the radical behaviorist is hard pressed to stretch his theory sufficiently.

Reward and Punishment

Let us accept, for the time being, the view that in the beginning physiological needs are all that are given. The mother of an infant is then in a very powerful position, since she can fully control the reward contingencies. One problem is that for a behavior to be either rewarded or punished (that is, strengthened or extinguished) it must first appear. It must also be a reasonably well-defined behavior over which the infant has some control. For example, a pigeon very early has not only a well-defined capacity to peck but the ability to direct its pecks accurately. Thus, if the experimenter wishes to induce a pigeon to peck a particular target, he has only to wait until the pigeon approximates the task and then immediately reward it with food. In due time, the pigeon will peck the chosen target rapidly and accurately. But while human neonates move a great deal, it is difficult to pick out a well-defined behavior over which they have reliable control. Thus the mother inclined toward behavior modification techniques as a method of child-rearing may be somewhat frustrated in the early weeks.

It seems entirely reasonable, however, that as the infant matures, its horizons expand to the point where mother as a person, because her presence is contiguous with food and body contact, is pleasant to have around. If being in the vicinity of mother becomes a reward, then increasingly controllable behaviors, such as vocalizations and smiling (which seem to help keep her nearby) will be increased in frequency. In this sense, the behaviorist's contentions are clearly supported, since it has been amply demonstrated in scores of studies that infants reared in barren, orphanage environments are far less mobile, reactive, and socially oriented than infants who receive much attention from loving parents. Whether these early effects of deprivation can be reversed is less well established (Yarrow 1968).

It is also not difficult to accept the view that, through a chain of conditioning, the mother—the source of food—becomes a generalized reinforcer, so that her mere approbation or disapprobation shapes the child's behavior. By the same process, reactions to the mother can be extended to all people, and social approbation in a more general sense becomes a reinforcement. The growing child conducts himself so as to increase behaviors approvable by all significant adults.

How does socially undesirable behavior then develop? The answer lies in the definition of the term "socially desirable." First, the family as a social microcosm may reward behaviors that are highly deviant or suspect in the broader world, and it may fail to extinguish behaviors that may be rejected elsewhere. Second, not all members of a family enter-tain the same views on what constitutes desirable behavior. To the extent that the father entertains expectations for the child's behavior different from the mother's and siblings different from either, the reward system for the developing child is likely to be somewhat confusing. Moreover, if the family is only indifferently representative of the larger community, the child's problems will be seriously compounded. Finally, any individual who is a social reinforcer in the child's environment may tend to be inconsistent. Adults and older children in a family may vary their be-havior toward a young child in ways consistent with the expectations of the outside world. To the child who cannot yet appreciate such sub-tleties of response, these demands are arbitrary, incomprehensible, and indistinguishable from the inconsistency produced by adult fatigue or impatience.

These inconsistencies and contradictions are, in the behaviorist's view, the primary source of anxiety. Anxiety, the feeling of apprehension and tension experienced when some response is necessary and no learned behavior is adequate to the need, occurs under any of several circum-stances. Anxiety is also defined as the feeling that occurs when acceptable problem-solving behavior seems to lead one into a fearful or ambiguous situation.

For example, suppose you must drive through a certain village on your way to work, a village with two traffic policemen. On the first day you are arrested for speeding. On the following day, therefore, you slow down as you approach the village limits, only to be arrested by the second policeman for delaying traffic. On the third day you speed up, and you are again arrested for speeding. By this time you are likely to be ex-periencing considerable anxiety since there apparently is nothing you can do to avoid punishment, yet you must drive through the village or risk losing your job. Suppose you then learn that the slow-down officer is on duty Mondays, Wednesdays, and Fridays, while the speed-up man is on duty Tuesdays, Thursdays, and Saturdays. On Sundays they alter-nate on an unpredictable schedule. Knowing this, you may recover from your anxiety on six days of the week, because you have discriminated a workable pattern of behavior and follow it. However, on those Sundays that require driving through the village, you will be just as anxious as ever.

Life circumstances frequently create extremely complicated learning situations requiring fine discriminations, and sometimes literally no be-havior is problem-solving. Consequently, everyone is subject to the ex-perience of mild to severe anxiety, rather often regardless of his efforts to learn the correct solution to problems quickly. Perhaps the most trying circumstances of all for the developing child are those in which he thinks he is engaged in correct, realistic, problem-solving behavior, and an explosion occurs in his social or physical environment. Since the child (and often adults as well) does not have a complete grasp of all of the contributing factors, he may make inaccurate assessments of causation. He may conclude that what he was doing at the time adults got into a furious argument or engaged in some other extravagant expressions of emotion in some sense caused the disturbance. This essentially innocent behavior would then become a source of anxiety to him.

At any rate, given this welter of confusing and contradictory reinforcements with consequent anxiety, it is difficult to understand how a child can ever develop into a rational adult who can cope with life. One possibility, which some behaviorists find unpalatable, is that the growing child, unlike lower living organisms, rather quickly develops some strategies for responding to the range of reinforcements in his social environment. In effect, the child decides, on the limited basis of his experience, which people under what circumstances he will permit to shape his behavior. The child's *cognitive* structuring of his social environment, accompanied by his tuning out some influences and voluntarily responding to others, does not preclude his being shaped by forces he has not taken into account in his scheme, or over which he has no control. However, many psychologists believe that only a theory that allows for internal structuring of experience by an individual will permit us to understand the coherency and consistency of behavior, and that exclusive dependence on a model of external reward and punishment will not.

The behaviorist, in response, would point out that one learned behavior has the effect of inhibiting the establishment of another learned behavior related to the same goal. Thus, the child is inexorably shaped with each increment in learning so that alternative reward-seeking behaviors become more and more difficult to induce. There is thus no necessity to postulate some internal monitoring apparatus to explain how people get set in their ways. The behavioral therapist would further assert that he has a demonstrable technique for teaching old dogs new tricks, and he would call upon the cognitive theorists to do as well with their techniques of modifying internal psychic structures. Moreover, the behaviorist would observe that where there are conflicting reward systems, behavior will ultimately be shaped by the stronger of the two—the earlier, most vivid, or most frequent. He would also point out that the context in which social reinforcement occurs can develop reward properties with or without the subject's awareness. If a situation is so highly ambiguous that the correct response is not evident, the subject may exhibit irresolution or visible anxiety. Or he may exhibit emergency behaviors such as flight or aggression.

Behaviorists believe that they can account theoretically for virtually any behavior by the combination of such learning theory concepts as classical and operant conditioning, reinforcement, secondary reinforcement, and generalization, coupled with special applications of reinforcement to produce inhibition or enhance discrimination, without recourse to hypothetical personality structures inside the individual. Thus behaviorists can explain misbehavior in a classroom, delinquent acting out, or any specific sick behavior on a psychiatric ward without hypothesizing intellectual or cognitive understanding. This is not to say that they can actually account for every given behavior exhibited by a person. Since they cannot know the detailed learning history of any individual, they do not pretend to have a better basis for reconstructing precisely the origins of symptomatic behavior than any other theorists. However, they assert that once they analyze what is sustaining unwanted behavior or inhibiting wanted behavior, they can set up a remedial program.

The advantage for therapy of a learning theory approach, the behaviorists repeatedly claim, is that their therapy is ahistorical; it does not depend on knowing or even hypothesizing how the client got the way he is. All the client has to do is indicate how he wants to be (provided he can specify his objectives in concrete terms), and the behaviorist can design a program to reduce or eliminate unwanted, uncomfortable, or socially unacceptable behaviors and increase the frequency of valued behaviors.

The specialist in behavior modification analyzes very precisely the circumstances under which a client experiences anxiety and then arrives at a diagnosis. He may decide that the client (1) has never learned certain essential social skills and must be trained in them, (2) has learned incorrect behaviors and must be retrained, (3) has made incorrect associations between two sets of events that should be severed, or (4) has not made adequate discriminations between two apparently similar but actually different situations. Social etiquette, for example, is largely based on discriminating between many superficially similar but actually quite different situations. It is generally considered a sign of friendliness to call a peer by his first name; it is considered a sign of brashness to call a superior by his first name without an express invitation to do so.

Symptom Formation

It should be clear by this time that behaviorists do not accept the view that symptoms are merely a superficial reflection of an underlying disorder. They take the view that emotional or behavioral deviation is not a disease in the medical sense of the term, but an indication of faulty learning. Since it is controversy over this issue that most sharply separates the behaviorists from most other theorists, it deserves some additional comment.

In psychodynamic theory, a symptom is always regarded as a reflection of a compromise solution to a psychosocial conflict. It is assumed that symptom formation occurs when a strong impulse cannot find direct expression because of equally strong social censure. In this sense it could be said that all behavior is symptomatic, since all overt behavior to some degree represents a compromise between the wish or impulse, constraints of reality, and constraints of conscience. However, the term "symptom," while covering a very broad range of physical, social, and psychological manifestations, is ordinarily reserved for compromises judged to be nonfunctional—where the impulse gains neither overt expression nor conscious examination.

For example, a young man may have a compelling sexual interest in a young woman who proves to be unamenable or unavailable. He might then seek out another woman, or masturbate, or take a cold shower and engage in vigorous exercise to divert his attention from sex. He thus acknowledges the impulse and makes the best compromise that his opportunities and moral scruples allow him. Another young man, with a similar impulse, may find an amenable girl but then prove to be impotent. Impotence is clearly a nonfunctional expression of a sexual impulse. From a psychodynamic standpoint, the symptom neatly resolves the young man's sexual conflict. We need not speculate about which of a variety of possible conflicts leads to impotence in this case. What is important is that psychodynamic theorists would think it necessary to uncover this conflict in order to resolve it and alleviate the symptom.

The behaviorist might conjecture about the factors in the client's conditioning history that led to the impotence, but this would be idle speculation, unrelated to treatment. The therapeutic task, simply and exclusively, would be to help the young man unlearn an inappropriate response and learn how to achieve and maintain an erection long enough to perform sexual intercourse. In short, the behaviorist believes an individual (1) learns psychopathological behavior just as he learns any other response, or (2) has failed to learn the appropriate response because he lacked opportunity or was actively discouraged in his attempts to do so. In the example given, it could be simply that assertive sexual behavior in childhood was repeatedly paired with punishment or social disapprobation. Thus, in all subsequent situations that might lead to sexual arousal the young man experienced more or less intense anxiety that precluded new learning.

A psychodynamic explanation of the same symptom would not necessarily rule out aversive conditioning of the sexual impulse, but would include the possibility that the symptom developed merely on the basis of fantasies of possible punishment, punishment that never occured in reality. Thus, in the classical dynamic explanation of the developmental psychology of the male, it is conjectured that a young child can develop a fear of injury by the father not because of any actual threat, but because the child's jealous, possessive attachment to the mother is in his own mind reason enough for the father to be aggressively angry. Failure to resolve this fantasied breach with father is judged to be consequential for the child's psychosexual development and an important determiner of his sexual capabilities as an adult.

The same general behavioral analysis could be made of any symptom: symptoms are no more than faulty learning that inhibits learning of more constructive alternatives. Such an approach can be rather appealing to a client who fears psychotherapy because he believes his symptoms reflect some hidden, highly demeaning aspects of himself which he prefers not to have revealed. For some obese people, for example, it is easier to seek help in correcting the habit of eating too much than to seek help for oral fixation, unconscious pregnancy fantasies, or deep-seated sexual problems—all of which have been offered as explanations of obesity by psychodynamic theorists (Weiss and English 1943; Fenichel 1945; Bruch, 1957).

THE METHODS OF BEHAVIORAL
THERAPY

There are two ways of applying learning theory to psychotherapy. One is to examine the work of traditional psychotherapists and demonstrate how their techniques can be understood in terms of unwittingly and inexpertly applied reinforcement principles. Krasner (1962), for example, has undertaken a thorough review of the contemporary literature on psychotherapy in order to demonstrate that the therapist, whatever his persuasion, is really a reinforcement machine. That is, regardless of what a therapist thinks he is doing, he is in fact doleing out social reinforcements, positive and negative. No matter how neutral in value judgments the therapist believes himself to be, he shapes the client's behavior in ways both subtle and direct and obvious.

A second approach is more direct. Behaviorists have devised their own array of techniques for treating emotional and behavioral disturbances. There are several well-developed and widely used techniques available to the behavior therapist. These include desensitization, relaxation, extinction following negative practice, avoidance learning, aversive conditioning, and operant conditioning. Some may be used alone or in combination, others have several variants, depending upon the problem to be solved.

Desensitization

Desensitization (Rachman 1966*a* and *b*) can be readily understood by observing the response of small children to animals. Initially, a young child may be fearful of a dog or other domestic animal, but if he is left alone with it or reassured by adults (and the animal is in fact not threatening), he will by slow degrees approach the interesting object. Once close to the animal, he will be reinforced by pleasure derived from play with a wooly, wiggly, affectionate object. Having been both desensitized to the animal's potential threat and reinforced by the pleasure derived from play and companionship, the child will be immune to fear, even if the animal engages in what the uninitiated would view as rather frightening behavior. Desensitization is an experience everyone has frequently in his life, since most new experiences have the effect of arousing some initial apprehension.

Negative Practice

Negative practice (Dunlap 1932) means simply that one deliberately practices producing errors in behavior until a high level of discrimination is achieved between the wrong and the correct behavior. This can be useful, for example, in the elimination of some firmly entrenched habits that contribute to low self-esteem. Suppose a person is so excessively apologetic and deferential in social situations that he induces people to reject him. A direct approach would involve training in self-assertion, but a useful adjunct might be play-acting cringing, apologetic behavior to the point where it is clearly discriminating from other, more adaptive social behavior already in the person's repertoire. Practice makes unwanted behavior stand out and sensitizes one to its incipient appearance.

Aversive Conditioning

Aversive conditioning has been widely used to gain symptom relief. The procedure requires the association of the symptomatic behavior with a painful stimulus until the unwanted behavior disappears. The technique has been most prominently used in the treatment of chronic alcoholism by the simple expedient of putting a strong emetic (Disulfiram, "Antabuse," emetine hydrochloride, or apomorphine) in the patient's whiskey (Hald and Jacobsen 1948; Dent 1954; Sargent and Slater 1954). Instead of separating the alcoholic from his liquor, he is urged to drink (in fact, he is required to do so by the contract he has with the therapist), but each time he drinks he is seized by an acute illness followed by retching and vomiting. If the cure works as it is supposed to, the alcoholic may become somewhat ill if he even looks at a bottle, and he will certainly be made highly uncomfortable by smelling alcoholic fumes. The technique has also been used with some success in treating sexual deviation by associating a painful stimulus with the inappropriate sexual object or act (Raymond 1956; Rachman 1961; Feldman and MacCulloch 1964; Barker 1965; and Feldman 1966).

Operant Conditioning

Operant conditioning (Skinner 1953; Krasner 1955) involves rewarding a person for a desired behavior at the time it occurs. It is the most frequent method used in training animals, but its application to humans presents some problems. If the subject is aware of what is taking place, he clearly can exert a choice about cooperating. As a graduate student, the author followed with interest an experiment some fellow graduate students were carrying out on (not with) a member of the faculty. This faculty member felt highly rewarded if students asked questions. He also tended to divide his time between sitting on the desk in the classroom and walking around on the low platform at the front of the room. The students decided to condition him by asking questions only if he was walking. In a matter of a few class sessions, they were able to increase his walking time very significantly. However, had someone informed the instructor of the nature of the experiment in which he was the guinea pig, he could easily either have frustrated it by remaining seated all the time or have turned the tables on the students by walking constantly and evoking from them an even higher emission of questions.

Just as desensitization is part of the experience of everyone, so is operant conditioning. By and large, all of us tend to emit rewarded behaviors at a higher rate than those that are not reinforced, and, in turn, we attempt to shape the behavior of others by expressing our pleasure or by providing more tangible rewards when they behave in a way that is gratifying to us. This being the case, in human transactions it is not always clear who is conditioning whom.

Sometimes we work out reciprocal arrangements ("I'll reinforce you, if you reinforce me"), and in other situations we like to see ourselves as slyly manipulating others with well-chosen, foolproof blandishments. Yet often an individual senses that he, the presumed operator, is being drawn into ambiguously gratifying situations by more or less subtle manipulation of this reward system by others. Among young adults the uncertainties about who pulls the strings in a boy-girl relationship have been examined in detail in countless plays, novels, and short stories. The boy casts out his line and the girl may pretend to bite, while in fact she is structuring her own strategies for shaping the behavior of her pursuer in ways he never intended.

Obviously, if one could manage the world of a client in such a way that only desirable behaviors gained favorable attention (or some other reward valued by him), it would be possible to shape his behavior very quickly. Unfortunately, outside the laboratory it is difficult to arrange matters in such an orderly fashion. Often a client's tentative efforts to gain approbation go unnoticed, while his unwanted symptoms continue to gain at least the reward of attention from others. The behaviorists, however, are quite correct in pointing out that therapists of whatever persuasion do behave in ways that reward some client behaviors while ignoring or punishing others. Thus a significant source of gain in all therapies may be the consistent approbation of the therapist of a client's successful efforts to alter a self-defeating behavior pattern.

Behaviorists believe that they can speed up the process by analyzing precisely which social environmental factors are sustaining the unwanted behavior and then altering the reward contingencies so as to eliminate the behaviors identified as symptoms. Some behavior therapists (or modifiers) do not act as therapists in the conventional sense of the term. Rather, they serve as technical consultants who analyze the problem and engineer its solution. The client himself (or the client and interested close relatives, friends, or associates) act the role of therapist by creating the altered structure of rewards in the client's environment. Some critics observe that in this effort to be scientific the behaviorist is giving too little attention to the generally rewarding nature of the interest, concern, and attention extended by the therapist trying to help the client (Andrews 1966).

One of the major criticisms leveled against behavior therapists has been that they focus almost exclusively on the treatment of well-defined, overt symptoms such as phobias, conversion reactions, enuresis, alco-holism, sexual disorders, speech disorders, and tension states, rather than the more diffuse problems of social and personal adaptation which practicing therapists believe they confront most often. The behaviorists' retort is that traditional therapists have simply ignored data such as when, where, with whom, and under what circumstances clients actually experience the complex problems of which they complain. Behaviorists assert that seemingly complicated sets of symptoms could, in fact, be broken down into discrete behavioral units manageable through use of one of the techniques based on learning theory.

RECIPROCAL INHIBITION THERAPY

Wolpe (1958) is perhaps the behavior therapist best known for techniques devised to cope with the client who presents many adjustment problems rather than one focal symptom. Called reciprocal inhibition therapy, Wolpe's procedure depends upon the belief that a condition of deep relaxation (often to the point of a light hypnotic trance) precludes the experiencing of intense anxiety. Thus, if a patient undertakes a vivid imaginary reconstruction of an anxiety-provoking situation while he is fully relaxed, it will not generate the usual anxiety. Wolpe assumes, as do many other theorists, that anxiety does not contribute to constructive problem-solving. Hence, reviewing a troublesome situation without the accompaniment of disorganizing anxiety permits a totally new perspective on it and enhances one's capacity to undertake a solution on a realistic basis.

Wolpe asks the client to list all his problems in a hierarchical order with the most anxiety-provoking at the top and the least anxiety-provoking at the bottom. The treatment sessions then proceed by first inducing deep relaxation and then taking the problems in reverse order. The relaxed patient is asked to imagine and describe as vividly as possible the anxiety-evoking situation that bothers him least. When he can relive this situation without experiencing anxiety, he moves on up the hierarchy, problem by problem.

The test of adequate recovery is a successful trial run in real life of the situations listed in the hierarchy. Not infrequently, the client will be free from anxiety in some situations he has worked on in therapy, but not in others. He can re-form the hierarchy, continue to reconstruct situations under deep relaxation, and then try again in the real situation. Wolpe and others who have adopted the technique (Lazarus 1963; Rachman 1965) claim a rate of recovery or marked improvement close to 90 percent, which is a considerably higher level of success than most studies of outcome report for other types of therapy. It is by no means certain, however, that Wolpe is using the same criteria of personal and social adjustment that are applied by others (see Breger and McGaugh 1965). But Wolpe has taken a major step toward meeting the criticism that behavior therapy cannot cope with the complex of personality problems, even though he is sometimes criticized as mechanical, superficial, and able to produce only short-lived relief of symptoms.

Since much of the essential research on major points of this controversy remains to be done, behaviorists and psychodynamicists are, for the most part, merely trading hostile assertions rather than offering cogent arguments based on generally accepted empirical findings. It is apparent, however, that behaviorists have interpersonal involvements with patients that probably have consequences not always taken into account in their strict learning theory models. Moreover, they ordinarily fail to reckon with the role of language in vivifying the fantasies and beliefs of their clients. For example, it is well known from medical research on placebos that what a therapist is doing is not nearly as important as what the client thinks or hopes the therapist is doing or is capable of doing (J. D. Frank 1959; Shapiro 1960). It is possible, for example, for a behaviorist to think he is relieving a symptom by using impersonal conditioning procedure, while the client is actually moved to change by his possibly fallacious perception of the therapist's loving concern about his difficulties. Psychodynamicists, on the other hand, are accused by behaviorists of wittingly or unwittingly applying behavior modification procedures while entertaining the belief that they are professionally neutral to the patient's disclosures.

AN EXAMPLE OF BEHAVIOR MODIFICATION

For purposes of further illustration, let us assume that Ginny (see McNeil 1967), whose psychoanalytic treatment we described in the previous chapter, had instead seen a behavior therapist. Ginny's manifest symptoms (chest pains, headaches, and stomach upsets) are not those commonly treated by behavior therapists. Nor are her chronic interpersonal difficulties with her mother or her conflicts about marriage readily approachable by simple conditioning procedures. Therefore we will assume that Wolpe's technique would be the treatment of choice.

It is clear what Ginny's life-long problem has been in behavioral terms. Her mother, for reasons that need not concern us here, has persistently and effectively used her hypochondriacal illnesses to manipulate Ginny's behavior with regard to independence and marriage. She simply became seriously ill and "threatened" to die if Ginny moved in any significant way toward independence. Thus, in order to achieve independence or to marry, Ginny would have had to sustain the intense anxiety associated with the idea of causing her mother's illness or even her death. Her mother's punishing behavior would not necessarily make independence less attractive, but it would make painful any move toward independence. If, in addition, as some mothers in similar situations do, Ginny's mother had systematically rewarded dependent behavior, Ginny's moves to be free of her mother might have been weakened over time and her conflict lessened.

The therapeutic task is to desensitize Ginny to her mother's threats and enhance the rewards of independence. The physical symptoms (with the exception of Ginny's chest pains) would present no serious problem, since they represent physiological reflections of intense anxiety and would disappear if the dependence-independence conflict were resolved. The chest pains, in contrast, may have been learned by modeling on her mother's device for managing others. Reluctant either to give up the possibility of marriage or to go through with it, Ginny might try to stop the flow of events by offering a valid physical excuse for temporizing. If her fiancé were to be impressed by this physical ploy, it would reinforce Ginny's use of chest pains to delay indefinitely the resolution of her conflict.

The behavioral therapist would first elicit Ginny's report of her current situation. He would then ask her to list in hierarchical order from the most to the least upsetting as many recurrent, anxiety-arousing encounters with her mother as she could. This rank order might include similarly anxious encounters with her fiancé. A hierarchy formed, the therapist would start with the least anxiety-arousing problematic situation—perhaps a situation in which some minor step toward independence was met by strong resistance from Ginny's mother.

Ginny would first be trained to achieve complete relaxation either by a method that systematically focuses on one muscle group after another (Jacobsen's technique) or by a light hypnotic trance. Completely relaxed, she would be asked to imagine the encounter with her mother as vividly as possible and to make it turn out differently. That is, she would be asked to imagine herself being assertive in the face of her mother's threats and resistant to her mother's efforts to arouse guilt. According to Wolpe's theory of reciprocal inhibition, Ginny's state of relaxation would make it difficult if not impossible to experience anxiety. Thus, she could become desensitized to her mother's manipulative operations.

By the time Ginny had been led through her hierarchy of anxiety-evoking encounters, she would, presumably, be able to confront her mother and assert her rights to independence (including marriage and the move to another city) with minimal anxiety. Free of the need to give in to her mother's threats, she would also be free to test more fully the potential delights of independence. If independent decision-making were to lead to gratifying experiences, the behaviors that comprise this orientation to self and others would be strengthened, and the possibility of a relapse would be reduced correspondingly.

There seems to be evidence that Ginny would find independence exceptionally gratifying. However, it is possible to conceive of instances in which independence might lead to punishing consequences. Adolescents, for example, are constantly torn between needs for dependence and needs for independence. Since adolescents are known to be impulsive on occasion, their expressions of independence sometimes lead them into disagreeable situations from which the only recourse is to flee back to dependency. The traumatic effects of this in-between stage might be greatly reduced if a cogent behavioral analysis of the period could be made and parents could thus be guided in assisting their children to reach independence by a series of graded steps.

Many parents complicate the lives of their children by inconsistent, thoughtless application of rewards and punishments. During the child's adolescence this problem is compounded by the wish of the emerging adult to participate in the manipulation of those pressures that govern his behavior. Ginny's mother made systematic efforts to punish independence. This led to her daughter's incapacity to make firm decisions regarding career and marriage without experiencing profound conflict and anxiety.

It is unfortunate that many behavior therapists have taken a polemical stance in their writing and that therapists of other schools are so often resistant to reexamining their own work in behavioral terms. Positions on both sides have become entrenched and have prevented an optimal degree of interchange. No one has yet undertaken a thorough, detached look at the spectrum of therapies with a view toward making a fair assessment and achieving a maximum reconciliation of conflicting views. Nevertheless, there seems to be little doubt that behavior therapists have pointed the way to a more rational analysis of the therapeutic task by defining problems, treatments, and outcomes in highly specific terms.

On the other side of the ledger, behaviorists have unfortunately tended to dismiss the subtle yet powerful effects on behavior of self-referent thoughts and silent speculation about others. Microanalysis of language and body movement may ultimately reveal objective, observable analogues to many internal processes. However, behaviorists will surely not gain widespread support for their position that the rather gross analyses of molar behavior they currently employ in defining problems and measuring outcome genuinely incorporate all that is relevant about the human experience. Acting in a confident fashion is not necessarily correlated with feeling confident; behavior of an affectionate sort is not always accompanied by loving feelings; obeying the law does not imply a felt sense of community that makes adherence to a set of consensually validated rules feel right.

Behaviorists are fully justified in pointing to the vagueness of definitions of terms in the current vocabulary of personality theory. They are also correct in suggesting that this vagueness contributes to our unfortunate tendency to enthrone concepts as if they were ultimate and absolute dicta. They are not justified, however, in pretending to a level of science they have not yet achieved simply by asserting that they have applied to psychotherapy established laws of learning derived in the laboratory. By overstating their cases, both sides of the current controversy are denying themselves the full benefit of a possibly fruitful collaboration.

A desirable scientific stance on the part of psychologists is that a theoretical position is no more and no less than a device to aid in organizing and interpreting empirical observations. Behavior theory, like the other theories presented in this book, is a set of premises and logically derived constructions that cannot be measured on a scale of absolute truth but only in terms of its utility. A basic tenet of the therapeutic approach based on learning theory is that modification of behavior occurs as a consequence of differential reinforcements. In the years ahead, we will acquire a clearer picture of the utility of this theory in the context of therapy by assessing the degree of success its practitioners achieve in the many emotional and behavioral problems to which it is now being applied.

Client-Centered Therapy

6

If someone seeking a compatible image of man is dismayed by the Freudian view of a perpetual struggle between powerful instincts and implacable social forces or repelled by the behaviorist's cool, detached, mechanistic stance, he may be attracted to Carl Rogers's basically optimistic view that we are all motivated by a quest for fulfillment of essential human values. In Rogers's terms, man is born with an *actualizing* tendency which, if it is not diverted or distorted by the vicissitudes of rearing, will eventuate in a *fully functioning* person. A fully functioning individual is characterized by self-knowledge, openness to new experience, and unshakable self-esteem. In contrast, a person who has been little valued in the course of his rearing, or has been confronted with unpleasant, uncompromising, or contradictory standards as a condition for receiving positive regard, will be hard pressed to maintain a stable identity in a basically incomprehensible or unfriendly world.

Whereas the fully functioning person is open to new experience, is reflective yet spontaneously reactive to himself and to others, and is capable of valuing others as well as himself, the maladjusted person is closed, rigid, and self-depreciating. It is important to note that in Rogers's opinion there is no evidence that man is inherently so self-seeking that he must be curbed by vigilant training and implicit or explicit threats of censure or punishment. An individual may be pushed off the path of self-actualization by unfortunate early experience, but if the pressure is released, his natural response is to return to the trajectory of life that is intuitively right for him, given his particular genetic endowment.

The client-centered therapist does not think of himself as a behavior modifier, nor does he regard himself as a tracer of instincts or an interpreter of unconscious motivation. Rather, he acts in such a way as to provide a client with the experience of being valued unconditionally, thereby freeing him of the necessity of organizing his behavior defensively in order to keep his anxiety within manageable limits. If experience confirms one's belief that the positive regard of others is contingent on behaving only in certain ways, then any tendency to behave in a contrary way is anxiety-evoking. The Rogerian therapist, by disconfirming the client's expectations, permits him to test out behavior and feelings that, although formerly proscribed, are experienced by the client as more genuine.

PRINCIPLES OF ROGERIAN THERAPY

Rogers (1965), the acknowledged originator and leader of the client-centered, nondirective school of therapy, is quite explicit about the personality theory on which his practice rests. He lists some nineteen propositions regarding the nature of man which he believes are to varying degrees supported by valid observations of human behavior. These are as follows:

1. *Every individual is the center of a constantly changing body of experience.*

Rogers qualifies this statement by noting that the portion of experience ordinarily symbolized in consciousness is but a fraction of that which is available if an effort of attention is exerted. There are countless thoughts, transient feelings, sensations, and perceptions just outside the range of fully conscious experience which can be moved to the foreground as needed. One concern of the client-centered theorist is that we understand that some experiences are prevented from registering in conscious experience even when they are important to the well-being of the individual. Another is that no matter how ingenious we may be in measuring a stimulus, we cannot, without the collaboration of the subject, know how that stimulus was actually experienced. In that sense, no expert can tell a client what he is experiencing and what it means; he can only invite the client to share with him the unique meaning an experience has for him.

2. *Reality is not a set of validatable events external to an individual but only what that person perceives and experiences.*

Rogers stresses that no two individuals see a person or situation in the same light. In an extreme situation an individual is termed paranoid because he interprets as malevolent, behaviors of others that are interpreted as quite innocuous by most other observers. Yet most of us have had the experience of differing sharply with an acquaintance in the evaluation of someone whom we both know well. Moreover, our behavior toward that individual is governed by this evaluation and usually changes only when a different interpretation is placed on the behavior that led to the original judgment.

3. *An individual responds as an organized whole to his world as he perceives it.*

This proposition underlines the interconnectedness of human experience and the consequent impossibility of altering one aspect of an individual's life without in some degree affecting all other aspects.

4. *The human has one overriding propensity, that of striving to maintain and actualize himself.*

Here Rogers emphasizes that the many needs and motives enumerated by psychologists are subordinate to the basic push toward self-realization. This proposition holds a central place in the client-centered theory of psychotherapy, for if there were no underlying directional striving toward self-fulfillment, it would be difficult to justify techniques aimed solely at enhancing self-disclosure.

5. *Human behavior is directed toward the goal of satisfying needs as experienced in the physical and social environment as it is perceived.*

Rogers leaves unresolved, because of the lack of acceptable evidence, the issue of whether or not needs such as affection or achievement are originally based on a biological inheritance. While he is inclined to believe that they are, his primary emphasis is on the rapidity with which such needs are elaborated and directed by the culture in which one lives. Moreover, the fact that some needs can be said to be genetically determined does not imply that behavior is dictated by them. It is the current tensions and needs *as perceived by the individual* that are motivational, not the biologically based needs he is born with.

6. *If emotion can be thought of as falling on a continuum between arousal (excitement, anger, fear) and quiescence (satisfaction, pleasure, calm), then the former is probably associated with exploring and overcoming barriers to need-fulfillment, while the latter is associated with achievement of a desired experience.*

The intensity of emotion, according to this view, depends upon the perceived importance of a behavior or sequence of behavior to maintaining and enhancing the self.

Propositions 7 and 8 draw attention to Rogers's concept of the self as a differentiated region of the total perceptual field and stress, as do a number of the basic principles, that the way to understand behavior is from the internal frame of reference of the individual.

It is of the highest importance to client-centered therapists to communicate to those whom they counsel that they will not evaluate, judge, or categorize. Rather, their total effort is devoted to perceiving the client from his own frame of reference. It follows from these propositions that, unlike most clinicians in a helping role, the client-centered therapist does not diagnose a client's condition. Diagnosis always carries with it an evaluation (How deviant in relation to a normative standard is this person's behavior?) and this is, moreover, a judgment imposed from the frame of reference of the expert. Rogers would insist that no matter how bizarre an individual's behavior may appear to the observer, one cannot ascertain its meaning without seeing the behavior through the eyes of the observed.

For example, a passenger in an automobile on a desert road may regard the driver as quite mad if, when they come upon a tumbleweed, he suddenly slams on the brake and drives into the ditch. Yet the driver's behavior is at least comprehensible if what he thought he saw was not a tumbleweed but a large boulder!

In Propositions 9 through 19, Rogers enlarges on deductions that follow logically from the postulation of the *self* as a more or less enduring organization of concepts, values, and perceptions of traits and relationships identified with *I* or *me*. He notes, for example, that the self is made up of both the reflected evaluative appraisals by others and the fruits of direct experience. Hence, the self may incorporate others' values, judgments, and perceptions as if they had been confirmed by experience when, in fact, they have not.

Rogers underlines the extent to which, early in life, we are almost totally dependent upon family members for the materials from which the self is constructed. If parents offer their child affection and secure support only on the condition that he modify his behavior and beliefs about himself in certain directions, then the child inevitably will do so. Behaviors or even thoughts designated as bad, unlovable, or stupid cannot be retained in the self-system. If, later in life, such behaviors are symbolized in consciousness, they are sensed as alien, while those aspects of self that have been consistently or strongly approved remain central. In this manner, values and beliefs that have never been tested by the actual experience of the child are nevertheless judged to be real.

Thus, as the personality develops, there is a continuous process of shaping new inputs so as to make them consistent with the organized body of experience already available. Any given new experience may be ignored because it is deemed unrelated to the self, taken in and integrated because it is deemed relevant, or denied expression in consciousness because it cannot be reconciled with the already-existing structure.

It follows that thoughts are translated into actions guided by and consistent with an individual's concept of himself. Nevertheless, since the self is only one aspect of the total sum of experiences, it is quite possible that an individual can act in a manner that he categorizes as not being himself. The mild-mannered person who erupts in raving anger when greatly provoked, or the stolid, unemotional person who is suddenly brought to tears by the misfortune of a friend, are illustrations of the intrusion into consciousness and behavior of affect and ideation categorized as *not me*. As we shall see, Rogers's concept of treatment involves expanding the client's self-concept so as to take in the maximum possible range of experiences. Any behavior, thought, or experience an individual actually has should not, in Rogers's view, be judged alien.

Indeed, in Principle 14, Rogers characterizes maladjustment, or a proneness to maladjustment, as a situation in which large areas of an individual's experience have been arbitrarily defined as inadmissible to the self-system. Other things being equal, the number of instances of thought and behavior experienced as alien and *not me* is in direct proportion to the total volume of experiences excluded from the self-concept. The degree of tension and anxiety experienced is roughly proportional to the frequency with which an individual experiences his own thoughts, feelings, and behaviors as alien and, hence, not really part of him and under his control. The common term, "self-possession," meaning calm and controlled, is close to Rogers's notion of adjustment as a state in which an individual is free of tension because virtually all his experience has been allowed access to the self-system.

In the last four principles (16–19), Rogers extends this general concept by noting that a self under threat by alien thoughts and feelings will try to strengthen its defenses and that only under conditions of reduced threat (that is, in the company of an accepting counselor viewed as an ally) can the defensive guard be relaxed. Once the process is reversed and the self is being enlarged by admitting previously excluded experiences, the process is self-sustaining. Not only is the client caught up in a continuing process of self-discovery, but, as a consequence of his own integration, he is more open to others—more capable of sharing their experience without anxiety and guardedness.

THE ROGERIAN COUNSELOR

Since Rogers's theory of personality has grown out of and remained closely identified with his therapeutic practice, the qualities required by a client-centered counselor are readily discernible. First of all, the therapist himself must have achieved a reasonably advanced state of integration of his experience into his self-system; otherwise he will not be open to accepting and comprehending the client's disclosures. By implication, he should also have been sufficiently widely and variously exposed to the viscissitudes of life so as to have broad areas of experience in common with his client. However, undefensive openness is far more important than mere congruence of life circumstances.

Second, the counselor must be capable of giving, beyond being merely nonjudgmental in the sense of refraining from delivering judgments. In Rogers's terms he must be capable of "unconditional positive regard" for his client; he must be capable of valuing another person without recourse to personal, abstract, or normative value systems. The helpful counselor must neither value the client simply because he or she is intelligent, beautiful, long-suffering, conventionally successful, wealthy, or of high social standing nor devalue the client without visible distinction. The stress is on *unconditional* positive regard, an attitude obviously, difficult to achieve in a world that trains people to draw invidious distinctions.

The counselor must also be sufficiently empathic to achieve *congruency* with the client's feeling state. Even though the therapist manages to maintain unconditional positive regard for his client, it would be difficult to proceed if there were no shared perception of feeling. Keeping in mind that minimization of threat to the client is essential, it is understandable that congruence is important. Few relationships are more implicitly threatening than those in which one's deep feelings are blunted by the other's incomprehension or cool neutrality.

Empathy is likewise a sine qua non for the spoken reflections of the therapist which, in the client-centered procedure, is virtually the only kind of intervention permitted. A reflection, far from being merely a parroting or rephrasing of the client's words as some critics of Rogerian therapy have suggested, is a response carefully chosen to illuminate a feeling implied in the client's communication but not actually stated. The entire forward thrust of the therapy depends on the capacity of the counselor to detect in the client's statements references to experiences, particularly feelings, that lie just outside his awareness and to articulate these experiences for the client in such a way that the self can be expanded to include them. A reflection that is off target or incorporates a wider range of feeling and content than the client is prepared to accept may make the client wary of offering further disclosures. A superficial reflection may not necessarily harm the relationship, but it does not move the client toward greater self-understanding.

To understand this important concept in client-centered therapy, it is important to clarify the difference between a reflection and an interpretation. An interpretation is an intellectual endeavor in which a therapist attempts to demonstrate a logical and lawful relationship between a number of disparate communications—verbal and nonverbal—from a patient. Whether an interpretation is correct or not is perhaps less important than the implication that the patient unwittingly communicates information about himself that only the expert can decode and clarify for him. The fact that only the expert can discern what the client is really saying or doing puts the client in a position of dependency, with much-reduced control over his own fate in the therapeutic process. A reflection, on the other hand, is aimed at saying no more or less than the client reveals about himself at the moment of speaking. The therapist, however, attempts to highlight what he understands to be the most poignant aspect of the communication. In this sense, the therapist does not purport to be an expert, although he may be a person whose normal perceptivity is enhanced by his having learned how to listen.

THE THERAPEUTIC PROCESS

Rogers and his co-workers, both at the University of Chicago and elsewhere, have been leaders in submitting the therapeutic process to empirical investigation. For this reason, while the theory of what should happen in client-centered therapy is not highly developed, evidence on what does happen is abundant. Following from Rogers's theory of personality we could conjecture that nondirective therapy might not have well-defined stages, but rather a somewhat predictable but uneven course toward greater self-awareness and self-satisfaction. This inference is based on the fact that the client, rather than the therapist, plays the major role in his quest for adjustment and determines the content of therapy sessions and the pace at which he will disclose feelings, thoughts, and information he deems consequential. While a client may achieve sudden, far-reaching insights in Rogerian therapy as well as in any other, the evidence does suggest a gradual shift in content and attitudes over the full period of the process.

Snyder (1945) and Seeman (1949), in their detailed analyses of several thousand client statements drawn from a number of examples of client-centered therapy, emerged with essentially similar findings. Initially, clients deal mainly with problems and symptoms, and the affective tone is negative. Later in therapy, clients reveal their understanding of connections between past and present behaviors and go on in the final hours to talk much more about present events and planned actions. The affective tone, meanwhile, changes from predominantly negative to predominantly positive. Rogers sees these findings as reflecting the client's movement from "symptoms to self" and from "others to self," from "past to present." Initially, the counselee is concerned with things that seem to be impinging upon him over which he has little control. Later he sees himself as much more central to the process of how his life will be lived and regards his wishes, feelings, and actions as being significant factors in the outcome.

Summarizing the research evidence, Rogers believes that the following statements on the process of nondirective therapy are, with some qualifications, justified. Early in therapy, the client is preoccupied with the focal problem that brought him into therapy; hence his affect is negative and his self-reference as well as references to others are consistently critical. The client's reports of current events reflect significant distortions, omissions, or unwarranted elaborations of self-referent meaning in the absence of confirming evidence. Alternative solutions to troublesome everyday problems are represented as limited, dependent on the whims of others, or doomed to failure.

In the middle stages there is a loosening of affect to the point where the client may seem to be in worse condition because he is more visibly upset by personal failures and frustrations or by the behavior of others. However, at the same time as he is much sadder when he is sad, he is also freed to be much happier in response to his own successes and to favorable behavior of others. The client dares to experience himself and others over a wider range, and thereby exposes himself to deeper injury just as he permits himself greater pleasure.

This opening of the self to experience—good and bad—is a necessary prelude to the final stages of therapy in which the client begins to regard himself as the master of his life rather than a perpetual victim. In the security of the relationship with his counselor, the individual who has shrunk from the full experience of which he is capable because experiment and risk were equated with intense anxiety now dares what he could not bring himself to do on his own.

Pallid emotional reactions, severely limited categories for construing events, a strongly evaluative approach to experience, and a highly conditional pattern of relationship with others are all characteristic of the person who experiences chronic unhappiness, tension, and a keen sense of being unfulfilled. While fortuitous intimate relationships with one or more relatively integrated, self-possessed people may have a therapeutic effect in the sense of freeing a troubled person in some areas of experiencing, the result, however satisfying, is always incomplete.

Thus, for example, an individual may become a valued member of a social group which not only condones but encourages a degree of freedom of expression much greater than that permitted by the person's family in childhood and adolescence. In the security of this group, he may share in the freedom with little anxiety, and hence be powerfully attracted to its members. At the same time, the option for being more open depends on group sanction rather than on a significant change in the self. For this reason, the changes a person makes are selective and often discontinuous with other aspects of self.

By contrast, in client-centered counseling, the client works his way toward freedom of feeling and action not through the sanction of the therapist but as a consequence of his having carefully and honestly questioned the necessity of his behaving and feeling in ways productive of so much dissatisfaction with self. New ways of experiencing and behaving achieved in this way belong more truly to the client, rather than being his on a franchise basis from a therapist, friend, or social group.

The successful client of client-centered counseling has many more categories and levels of experience available to him. He is far less critically evaluative of those he encounters, since he has much less guilt in establishing and breaking off relationships on a realistic basis. He can actually take pleasure in the experiences and ways of others even though they differ significantly from his own life style. Above all, he has a sense of enjoying himself, of taking pleasure in his thoughts, feelings, and actions and in his greatly enhanced sense of choice.

Curiously, a person greatly helped by therapy—and this among other factors makes measurement of outcome difficult—may be perceived by others who have known him over a period of time as worse in at least some respects. He may be seen as more volatile, less reliable, more self-centered, more demanding, and so on. To be sure, individuals sometimes enter therapy because they perceive themselves to be overemotional, inconsistent, unreliable, and narcissistic. In such instances, if these characteristics prove to be defenses against insecurity and anxiety, then successful therapy should lead to moderation in these areas. A majority of clients, however, are troubled by problems such as timidity, restraint, self-subordination, and compulsive attention to rules, regulations, and the expectations of others. Those who are associated with the client may have found no fault with such an array of characteristics and would not be altogether pleased if they were less prominent. Sponsors of individuals entering therapy are usually willing to accept reduction of such unpleasant symptoms as depression, intense anxiety, irritability, inability to work, chronic fatigue, or headaches, but they are usually not prepared to accept significant personality changes.

A CASE THERAPY

Since Rogerians have neither an elaborated technique, a clearly defined set of subgoals making up therapeutic stages, nor a vocabulary for talking about clients as objects, it is not easy to describe the therapeutic process short of creating an entire therapeutic dialogue. Indeed, training in client-centered counseling and any discussion of current cases in a treatment center adhering to that orientation are closely tied to recorded transactions between therapist and client. No case is conceptualized in such a way that the therapist develops a confident view of the big picture which he shares with the client as he sees it. In the same way that Rogerians eschew diagnosis, they also reject the utility of genetic explanations adduced by the therapist. Consequently, a supervisor of a therapist-in-training or a trained therapist reviewing his own work concentrates on how sensitively and accurately the therapist caught the feeling latent in each of a sequence of client statements.

Based on our knowledge of Ginny's long-standing conflict with her mother, we can anticipate that she would spend a great deal of time in the first hours defining her difficulty in breaking away from her mother's influence in order to be married. She would describe how sad she feels that life is slipping away from her and castigate herself for being weak, dependent, and easily intimidated. Ginny would also criticize her mother for being so domineering, unfair, and selfish; her father for having been so weak and hence failing to protect her.

Key exchanges around these issues might go as follows:

GINNY (angrily): Just about every time in my life that I have tried to do something *I* wanted to do when and how I wanted to do it, my mother would either criticize my plans until I gave them up or, if that didn't work, she would become very ill because of my obstinacy. Then I would get scared.

THERAPIST: It seems to have been very upsetting to you to learn that you had the power to make your mother ill.

GINNY: Yes, it was very upsetting, but sometimes it seems that mother is just using her illness to keep me tied to her.

THERAPIST: So even though it often seems as if it is your behavior that is affecting your mother's health, you sense that it is really she who is controlling you.

GINNY: Yes, but it would still be terrible if I somehow caused her death.

THERAPIST: Deep down you are really frightened by the thought that you actually could kill her by opposing her.

. . . .

GINNY: About my fiancé and the plans for marriage, I feel all mixed up. I love him and want to marry him. I'm embarrassed that I appear so changeable and uncertain. Yet at the same time I'm angry because he doesn't seem to be sympathetic with the spot I'm in with my mother. He ought to be more patient while I work things out.

THERAPIST: You would really be relieved if your fiancé saw your problem with your mother in the same way you do.

GINNY: In one sense, maybe. In another, I like his ability to make firm decisions and stick with them. He seems stronger than my father was— my father always gave in to my mother. But I'm just not ready to take the leap of both marrying *and* leaving the city when my mother is so opposed.

THERAPIST: You really feel as if the two people most important to you are tearing you apart.

GINNY (sadly): Yes.

Later in therapy one might conjecture an exchange as follows:

GINNY: Still, when I think back, I have accomplished a good deal in spite of my mother. I've been away from home and on my own twice and really enjoyed it when I could stop thinking about how reproachful my mother would be if she knew I was enjoying myself. My mother complained endlessly about her health, but nothing actually happened to her when I went away from her.

THERAPIST: You believe that once *you* have the courage to oppose your mother, she may accept it better than she says she will.

GINNY: Yes, I see that it is *really* my *own* lack of conviction about what is the right thing to do that holds me back. In this sense, I blame my mother for a fault that is at least half mine.

Then, toward the end of the therapy, one might hear the following:

GINNY (cheerfully): Well, it's all set. I'm leaving in two weeks to be married.

THERAPIST: Finally making the decision really makes you pleased with yourself.

GINNY: It certainly does. I've talked everything over with my fiancé, and he agrees that mother can visit us from time to time. Meanwhile, I've talked with her doctors—something I could never bring myself to do before—and they tell me that basically she's in very good health for a person of her age. She is bitching a lot, but I just tell her that I've decided and that's it.

THERAPIST: It is really a relief to have reassurance about her condition even though you suspected she was exaggerating.

GINNY: Yes, it certainly is. But I couldn't really bring myself to find out until I had solved my own problem about being independent. As long as I needed her, I had to believe she really needed me.

THERAPIST: Yes, that certainly seems to be the way it is.

We see in these short, illustrative exchanges Ginny's original dysphoria and self-criticism give way to a more realistic appraisal of herself and finally to a self-satisfied planning for the future. The therapist, true to his theory, stayed with Ginny as closely as he could. He did not reassure her when she was self-depreciating, nor did he attempt to interpret her mother's or her fiance's behavior to her. Rather, the therapist showed complete respect for the client's capacity to bring out and effectively confront any thoughts, feelings, and attitudes that were creating emotional turmoil.

The therapist's respect for his client's push toward fulfillment and for her ability to understand herself without depending upon the therapist's superior knowledge is a keystone of the Rogerian position and is perhaps unique to this position. Unlike other therapists, the client-centered therapist takes no responsibility for the outcome except insofar as he is responsible for extending unconditional positive regard, empathy, and congruence to the client, the last referring to reflections that are really in tune with the client's communications rather than off target.

Rogers believes that the general principles that underlie his therapeutic approach are widely applicable to teaching, supervision, and, indeed, in any social interaction. In his current work at the Western Behavioral Sciences Institute, he is attempting to make further extensions of his theory into community action programs.

Other Forms of Therapy

In the foregoing chapters, we have described in some detail the three most commonly practiced forms of therapy that follow from three different conceptions of man. There are many other reasonably well-articulated theories of psychotherapy, some of which endorse rather distinctive practices. In this chapter, we shall give summary descriptions of several of these therapies and merely identify several others which are currently represented by very few practitioners.

THE INTERPERSONAL THEORY OF PSYCHOTHERAPY

The theory and practice of Harry Stack Sullivan (1947, 1953, 1954) continue to be influential because, during his lifetime (he died in 1949), he was instrumental in the establishment of two training centers, one in Washington, D.C., and the other in New York City. Although the most devoted adherents of Sullivan are found mainly on the East Coast, his ideas are widely known, respected, and have been incorporated in other bodies of theory and practice—often without full credit to the originator.

Sullivan has asserted that not only do those characteristics that are singularly human result from the countless transactions with others from birth, but personality is in effect those durable characteristics manifested in interpersonal "fields of force." Although humans share with other animals a capacity to experience fear, only humans experience anxiety, in Sullivan's meaning of the term. Situations evoking fear are generally susceptible to analysis, and in some instances habituation is possible. The events that precipitate anxiety, however, are characteristically obscure, because an effect of anxiety is a marked reduction in capacity for accurate observation and analysis. All humans are subject to anxiety in varying degrees. Hence they devote a great deal of often fruitless effort to achieving security—to warding off that uncanny feeling which, according to Sullivan, has its origins in the earliest empathic communication of an infant with a mother who is herself angry, anxious, or fearful from time to time. Since human identity is rooted in recurrent relations with others, man is driven to avoid loneliness and to satisfy needs through others. But these efforts are at the expense of exposure to anxiety.

Sullivan's formulation is not strikingly different from that of other theorists, but a therapeutic intervention conducted in accordance with Sullivanian views does focus on a set of data different from that viewed as important by other schools. First of all, the therapist is regarded as a participant observer—as a social scientist, if you will, rather than as a healer. From his vantage point as a participant—and, at the same time, a somewhat detached expert observer—in an ongoing interpersonal process, the therapist is able to detect aspects of the client's verbal and postural behavior of which the client is not aware. Concurrently, the therapist can note the content and type of communications of the client and draw reasonable inferences regarding the probable sources of difficulty he is experiencing in resolving interpersonal integrations (that is, relationships defined by the actor's needs).* The client's actual relationship with the therapist is, of course, under scrutiny, along with those reported by the client.

There are three tactics in therapy that Sullivan judges to be conducive to helping a patient: (1) clarifying in considerable detail the actual interpersonal situations in which unfortunate outcomes repeatedly occur; (2) using these areas of disordered function as a starting point to examine less obvious effects of the disorder on other areas of living; and (3)

---

* Sullivan postulates three modes of experience and communication: prototaxic, parataxic, and syntaxic. The prototaxic mode is associated with infancy and the totally involving experiences and responses that are characteristic of an undifferentiated organism. In the adult, remnants of this mode may be reflected in encompassing "oceanic" feelings which are difficult to describe or account for. The stark terror of the person on the edge of an acute psychotic break may be considered an experience in the prototaxic mode, as, indeed, may be some experiences under the influence of LSD. Parataxic experience and communication may be coherent and logical, but it is experience erected on an incorrect premise. Any time one responds to another person not in terms of how he actually behaves but in terms of strongly emotionally toned and incorrect expectations, he is said to be communicating in the parataxic mode. The syntaxic mode is one in which the premises are valid and the derivations logical and coherent.

consolidating understanding of current disorders in living by tracing origins of inadequacies in development to experiences with significant others of the past.

Sullivan regards the psychiatric interview as being divisible into (1) the formal inception, (2) the reconnaissance, (3) the detailed inquiry, and (4) the termination. These stages might also describe an extended therapeutic encounter, since each segment—particularly the reconnaissance and detailed inquiry—can be expanded as necessary. In identifying these stages, Sullivan reveals his concern with establishing the identity of both the expert participant observer (the therapist) and the client. He wants the client to have an explicit understanding of the contract he is entering into. That is, he wants to make certain that the client is really seeking a psychotherapist—an expert on troubled interpersonal relationships—rather than some other kind of specialist, and that the nature of his difficulties justifies the use of the therapist's particular skills. Sullivan is then concerned with the therapist's obtaining as much accurate information as he can on who the client is and how he came to be that way. The reconnaissance, or history, leads naturally into a detailed inquiry into the focal current problems presented by the client.

Unlike many therapists, Sullivan recommended that the client be given a task to perform between sessions—to recall a particular event in greater detail, for example, or to look more closely into recurrently troublesome relationships with significant people in his life. Thus, Sullivan supported a rather crisp, structured, straightforward, goal-oriented, no-nonsense approach to therapy. Unlike the client-centered therapist, he viewed himself as an expert who, with sufficient data, could make valid, helpful observations that would usefully expand the client's range of knowledge about his interpersonal operations. Unlike the Freudian psychoanalyst, he believed he could intervene constructively and definitively in some problem areas without necessarily reconstructing all the stages of the client's psychosexual development by means of transference. Indeed, he did not think of therapy as involving a definitive and complete cure, but only as a lesser or greater mitigation of troublesome anxiety-provoking experiences. These views of the process of therapy, together with his particular focus on communication in the context of significant interpersonal encounters, make his contribution quite distinctive.

EXISTENTIAL PSYCHOTHERAPY

Rollo May (1958) is perhaps the best known among a growing number of American exponents of existential psychotherapy, but the movement in which he participates has a direct line of descent from such distinguished European practitioners as Viktor Frankl, Ludwig Binswanger, and the Swiss-born Henri Ellenberger. Since the theory and practice is explicitly rooted in and derived from a philosophic position, it is important to take a brief excursion into his antecedents.

It is possible to define all therapies as ways of knowing, in terms of one or another basic philosophic orientation. Specifically, this means that it is vital to know how the problem of knowing other persons as well as ourselves is defined and set forth. What is the theoretical or philosophic status of the *person?* Who is he? What is he? How is he differentiated from other objects in a world full of objects?

Schools of thought in philosophy can be basically divided into materialist and idealist, or realist and idealist, or positivist and humanist. For modern thought, phenomenology is the predominant version of the view that essential reality lies in consciousness. It has been, one way or another, the source of all psychologies that reject the possibility of man's being studied as an object. Scientists generally take the position that whatever is knowable is outside of consciousness, in nature, waiting to be discovered. Whatever is there to be discovered can be found by anyone with the techniques and patience to do so. The phenomenologist, however, argues that whatever may be "out there" in nature is not ultimately knowable. All that can be known are the perceptions and thoughts of the discoverer. *Just because* we are active participants in the world— interpreting it, acting upon it, changing it—our relation to the world is different from that of stones or trees or stars or atoms. An interaction theory of knowledge led, then, to an emphasis on the active role of the knowing, perceiving person. It also led to new emphases on interpersonal or social relationships, our knowledge of other persons, and, of course, our knowledge of ourselves.

Existentialist psychologies are based on these themes. Antibehaviorists applaud the reality of subjective feelings and experience; antipositivists proclaim the different and autonomous sphere of persons as distinguished from other physical objects. These psychologies tend to be voluntarist and antideterminist—the person as an active being is not merely a subject in the world at large, but formally free to involve himself in it, change it, and act upon it. Thereby he becomes an agent who determines events and is not just determined by them, engaging himself, not just sitting by.

Psychological theory and philosophic positions originating in Europe generally undergo substantial modification when they are interpreted and applied in the United States. The roots of contemporary phenomenology can be found in Edmund Husserl's attempts in the early 1900s to find a basis for logic and epistemology in experience, but Husserl's

144   PSYCHOTHERAPY

concerns have little in common with those of psychologists intent on
creating a new frame of reference for psychology in opposition to the
objective, positivist tradition of the behaviorists. There is perhaps in the
literary-philosophic cult of nihilism and pessimism popularized by Jean-
Paul Sartre in France after World War II a more direct connection
between European existential-phenomenological thought and current existential therapies. Sartre holds that each man exists as an individual in
a purposeless universe and that he must oppose his essentially hostile
environment by exercising his free will. Man cannot expect to find
meaning in the external world but only in his own directed acts. Neither
nihilism nor pessimism was likely to capture the enthusiasm of Americans
who have traditionally regarded themselves as buoyantly optimistic and
forward-looking. Neither have Americans been prone to view the environment as necessarily hostile. What remains when these two elements are
removed is the rather general proposition that, while man is powerfully
motivated to seek meaning for his existence in something outside himself,
he must ultimately find it within himself and through his acts. Instead of
seeking meaning, on the one hand, in religious or political dogmas and
cultural prescriptions or, on the other, in the fundamental pleasures to
be found in expression of instincts inherited from our animal ancestors,
one taps those elevated capacities in himself that are uniquely human
and are fully known only engaging in experience—being "in the world."

May identifies some six characteristics by which existential therapy
can be distinguished from other approaches. He notes that technique
per se is identified with seeing the client as an object. Hence technique
should be subordinated to understanding and follow rather than precede
understanding. Existential therapists, therefore, are more variable in
their techniques and never follow a procedure simply because it has
the support of tradition or custom. Technique is flexible and must be
adjusted to the needs of the individual client. The guide to technique
is the question, What will most effectively disclose the existence of this
particular client at this particular point in his life?

A second characteristic is the emphasis on "presence": the therapist
and the client are two live people in a real relationship. This is in contrast to the classical Freudian view of the therapist as a mirror who merely
reflects what the patient projects but consistent with the Sullivanian notion of the therapist as a participant observer. The therapist does not
interpret events in therapy so much as he demonstrates them through
his relationship with his client. Thus, so-called transference phenomena
are not explained away as having nothing to do with the person and
behavior of the therapist but are brought fully within the relationship
and viewed as contemporary acts toward and with the therapist.

A third identifying feature is that psychological dynamisms are not viewed as a kind of species-specific behavior common to all humans and therefore lacking uniqueness. A client's dynamics are understood as deriving their unique meaning from the context of his life. Forces held in repression are viewed simply as potentials of which the client has not yet been able to avail himself. The therapist does not always know what is really motivating the client. He listens with seriousness and respect to the client's communications rather than looking beyond or around them for a pat explanation based on formal theory.

By the same token, the therapist undertakes to analyze any ways of behaving—his own or the patient's—that serve to dilute or destroy "presence." Empty interpretive formulae, technical rigidity, social forms that create distance—all these have a potential for compromising the reality of the confrontation of patient and therapist and must therefore be brought up for deliberate scrutiny when they are detected.

The objective of existential therapy is to increase the patient's consciousness of his own existence and thereby to help him *experience* his existence as *real*. The intent is to heighten the patient's sense of continuous, self-directed involvement and movement, in contrast to a feeling of simply being reactive to external events in an episodic and discontinuous manner. Thus, the therapist may be less likely to inquire how a client is—as a member of a healing profession does—but where a client is in terms of his direction and involvement.

Finally, existential therapy is characterized by the importance attached to commitment. To the existentialist, a person is not alive if he is not unconditionally committed to something. Truth exists only as it is revealed in action, and knowledge is not the precursor of decision but a consequent. For this reason, therapy cannot be construed as a moratorium on decision-making or a retreat from commitment. Obviously, existential therapists do not routinely encourage impulsive leaps into decisions of far-reaching importance. Yet they do quite firmly and unequivocally observe that man is mortal and that the certainty of death is what makes each living hour something of absolute value.

NEOPSYCHOANALYTIC THERAPY

Just as immigrants are altered by their immersion in the culture of their adopted homeland, so are psychotherapeutic theories and practices modified by transplantation to the United States. Freudian psychoanalysis, safeguarded as it is by the several institutes of psychoanalysis, has nevertheless undergone substantial change over the years, particularly in its increasingly heavy emphasis on ego function in contrast to an earlier concern with instinctual drives and the id.

Some influential psychoanalysts took issue with Freud long before psychoanalysis was established in the United States. Jung, Rank, and Adler are perhaps the most famous of Freud's disciples who broke with the master and created their own schools of thought. However, with the possible exception of Adler, they have had relatively little influence on the training of therapists in this country and therefore have few followers.

Karen Horney, (1937, 1939, 1942, 1945, 1950) on the other hand, although less well known, was one of the founders of the American Institute of Psychoanalysis in New York City, as well as an influential early member of the Association for the Advancement of Psychoanalysis. She came to the United States in 1932 and, until her death twenty years later, was a very active and highly respected teacher. Many currently practicing therapists reflect her point of view in their work and continue to teach her theories. Horney discarded Freud's instinct-based developmental theory in favor of a psychology based on the characteristic conflicts and frustrations experienced by a child in a particular social and cultural setting. Like Sullivan, instead of regarding a neurosis as a largely intrapsychic phenomenon, she saw it as a reaction to deprivation of parental warmth and affection expressed in interpersonal relationships.

Children, she theorized, are propelled by a basic anxiety, which is a reflection of their repressed hostility toward parents, who impose stringent conditions of behavior in exchange for expressions of affection. In order to minimize this basic anxiety, humans must move against, toward, or away from others in a calculated, even compulsive manner, rather than spontaneously. Faced with dependency on parents and other adults, who demand concealment of the real self as the price for acceptance, the child creates a fictive, idealized self, for which unrealistic claims are made and in which he has enormous, although false, pride. Clearly, the more unrealistic the claims made in support of the fictive self, the deeper the hatred toward the real self, which stands as a constant rebuke to falsification (or idealization) of feelings, values, and abilities. The neurotic lives in perpetual fear of being unmasked and hates not only his real self but others who threaten to expose the confidence game he is perpetually playing.

For example, if a person had carefully constructed an image in which his power and competitive ability were idealized, he would hate any sign of weakness in himself, go to great lengths to disguise it, and would be made intensely anxious and angry if those around him threatened to deflate him, even in trivial ways. People close to him would be trained to acknowledge his pretended superiority, or they would suffer the effects of his vindictive pride. Another person, who organized his image around a fiction that he needed no one and could remain indefinitely happily aloof and distant from others, would hate any sign of need for affiliation or dependency in himself, and would be made anxious if others detected such needs.

Because of cultural pressures exerted through the family, women often develop an idealized self, organized around a putatively unqualified affection for husband and children. They are self-abnegating and seem wholly devoted to serving the needs of others. A woman with such a fictional self-image abhors any indication of selfishness in herself and is made anxious if others suggest that they are giving her anything— attention, affection, or compliance to her wishes—because she is covertly controlling and demanding.

Therapy following from Horney's theory is a form of character analysis. The therapist invites the patient to review his life and particularly his current significant relationships from the standpoint of uncovering the illusions on which his wishes, feelings, values, and typical behavior are based. He is asked to give up his false pride and rediscover his "real" self and his "real" conflicts. Needless to say, the patient, despite the pain of the anxiety and the symptoms that brought him to therapy, strongly resists giving up the fictions that seem to give his life a degree of coherence and give him a sense of worth.

Healing, according to Horney, occurs more or less spontaneously, once the obstructive character defenses are removed. In this sense, character analysis does not differ significantly from other contemporary modes of treatment. In virtually all forms of therapy (Jungian analysis may be an exception), the emphasis is on the removing of impediments to self-awareness and personal growth. It is assumed that synthesis and constructive application of new insights are the responsibilities of the patient. He is presumed to be free to live his life and express himself in his relationships with others in a manner consistent with his now-revealed genuine personal needs.

This conception of therapy is in marked contrast to one in which the effort is to free the patient of characteristics that prevent him from meeting standards of membership in a saving community. For example, many religious groups have devised techniques for assisting deeply conflicted, anxious individuals to perfect themselves and thereby achieve eligibility for admission to a circle of "saved" people.

The technical procedures of character analysis exemplified in Horney's approach, in contrast to the theoretical views, are essentially no different from other analytic therapies. Horney was trained in a Freudian psychoanalytic institute in Germany and, since her interest was not in technica. innovation but in theory-building, it is not surprising that it was mainly at the conceptual and interpretive level that she differed from her more conservative colleagues.

RATIONAL PSYCHOTHERAPY

The average layman views psychotherapy mainly as a device for straightening out one's thoughts about personal problems. His experience with nonprofessionals from whom he has sought counseling leads him to believe that another person can sometimes be useful in pointing out flaws in one's analysis of a difficult situation. Moreover, others can often perceive possible solutions which one's own biases block out.

Albert Ellis (1962) is one of the few theorist-practitioners in the post-Freudian era to give professional sanction to the layman's view that irrational approaches to personal problem-solving can be treated directly by examining the logical fallacies on which self-defeating behavior is based. Ellis proposes that man is naturally oriented toward harmonizing his self-interest with his social interest but that, in the course of his rearing, he may be induced to accept without question any number of demonstrably false premises. If the premises on which he bases his views of himself and others are incorrect, then he cannot fail to be repeatedly disappointed in outcomes of relationships with others. He will be driven to solve problems by emoting rather than by deliberate, calm analysis.

Ellis does not reject the observations of Freud and other theorists who locate the origins of illogical thought and behavior in the child's earliest relationships in the family. The child develops false premises about himself and others because they are imposed upon him. However, he asserts that Freud paid too little attention to what sustains such illogical thoughts and how they might be altered in the interests of the patient. Speaking very generally, most psychoanalytic therapists do assume that ego functions improve spontaneously once the unconscious conflicts and distortions are revealed in the transference relationship. By the same token, psychoanalysts regard it as utterly fruitless to attack a patient's irrationality with logical argument.

By contrast, therapists using rational analytic techniques believe that they can directly challenge irrational thought and behavior where they find it. If the patient rigorously monitors his thought, with guidance from the therapist he can sort out the false premises on which his life style is based and thereby escape the emotional turmoil that persistently accompanies improper, inadequate, or incorrect analyses of problematic

ife situations. In effect, Ellis is saying that thought and emotion are two
ides of the same coin, and therefore if one thinks rationally his emo-
ions will be manageable sources of gratification rather than a chronic
hreat to his personal and social well-being. Put another way, emoting
s a kind of disordered, biased, evaluative way of thinking that precludes
he comparisons, discriminations, and refined judgments that lead to the
best possible resolution of a given problem.

The ten guiding principles underlying Ellis's therapy (1958) suggest
some considerable influence from the existential-phenomenological-hu-
manistic camp. For example, he asserts that man is free and should define
himself, that he should cultivate his individuality, that he should live in
dialogue with his fellow man, and that man's experiencing should be his
highest authority for action. He urges full awareness of the immediate
moment and asserts that there is no truth except in action. At the same
time, he advises accepting certain limits in life even though one should
live creatively.

The effective therapist, according to Ellis, should be untiring in un-
masking his client's illogical thinking and self-defeating verbalizations by
demanding that the client focus his attention on such lapses and reconstruct his logic. The therapist should support the client by tracing out
how illogical thinking is maintaining his disturbance and unhappiness
and by teaching him techniques for analyzing and rethinking problematic areas of living.

Of particular interest in Ellis's system is the therapist's continuing
with a client beyond the rooting out of the particular logical distortions
supporting the particular disturbances that brought him to therapy. Ellis
again reflects his philosophic bent by asserting that the therapist has a
responsibility for inoculating the client against a whole series of fallacies
endemic to our culture. He hopes to help the patient avoid not only the
logical pitfalls to which he fell heir as a consequence of his particular
life circumstances but also those prevalent illogical ideas that might
attract him in the future.

The following twelve admonitions (somewhat paraphrased from Ellis's own words), although not exhaustive, are representative of the rational therapist's guide to sensible living:

1. Do not believe that you have to be loved or approved by everyone
   for everything you do. Seek such approval as is necessary to achieve
   your own purposes (which should be directed at enhancing self-
   esteem). Concentrate on loving rather than on being loved.
2. Reassess your judgment regarding behaviors that you categorically
   regard as wicked and punishable. View people (including yourself)

who perform inappropriate or antisocial acts as ignorant, unintelligent, or emotionally disturbed—not bad.

3. Try to change for the better things you can control, but accept the fact that there are many conditions over which you cannot prevail and to which you must become resigned. [Obviously, it is rather important to be able to distinguish accurately which life events fall in which category.]

4. Virtually all unhappiness is a product of (or is sustained by) the view one takes of events. No-one or no set of external events forces you to be unhappy.

5. Face dangerous or fearful situations directly and frankly with the intention of reducing their threat. If you cannot change the situation, do not dwell on it (see 3 above).

6. Running away from difficulties is, in the long run, the self-defeating choice. [The implication here appears to be that one cannot escape from problems since they are largely internal and will emerge again and again until they are faced directly.]

7. Stand on your own two feet. No one *needs* something or someone to lean on, however much one may wish for a comforting, dependent relationship. One must exercise one's initiative and ability if he is to gain faith in himself.

8. Doing is more important than invariably doing well. One need not be uniformly competent, but one must accept limitations and imperfections in order to make the most of genuine talents.

9. One should learn from past experience but not be wedded to it. Yield in a discriminating way to contemporary influences and experiences rather than holding tightly to the lessons learned in the past. No matter how strongly something has affected you, it need not affect you indefinitely.

10. Do not try to change people with direct, urgent pleas. What other people do is not as vitally important to one's well-being as one often thinks. Other people's deficiencies are *their* problems, and pressure will not help them.

11. Humans are happiest when they are actively and personally involved in creative undertakings or devoting themselves to others.

12. Emotions can be controlled if one practices saying the right kinds of sentences (that is, logical rational observations) to himself.

There is something a bit quaint about this impressive array of good thoughts—rather like all the avunclear advice ever uttered being brought together in one long sermon. Advice is easy to offer and hard to follow—as item 10 indicates—but in the hands of a skilled rational therapist the list is more likely to be used not in direct suggestions but as a guide to

amiliar rationalizations that slip into the client's communications—de-
ensive verbalizations which can then be rigorously tested.

Nevertheless, the rational psychotherapist is very direct, active, and, by
mplication, a bit preachy. He serves as a frank counter-propagandist
who contradicts, denies, challenges, and even scorns the self-defeating
superstitions the client has originally learned and internalized. Moreover,
the therapist "encourages, cajoles, and at times commands" the client to
do what is good for him—namely to think rationally in the context of
a rational philosophy.

A therapy, which is active and meets the client's problems at the level
at which he is experiencing them, is likely to be favorably received. The
unsophisticated client expects to have his views questioned by the therapist and to receive usable advice from the knowledgeable expert. The
rational analyst provides both in abundance.

Therapists of most other schools are generally trained to be relatively
passive, to let the client talk, and to intervene mainly to expand in a
subtle way the range of the client's observations about himself. Often
this approach leaves the client who is unfamiliar with therapy with the
uneasy feeling that the therapist either has nothing to offer or that he does
not accept the patient's statement of his problem at face value. Some
research (Heine 1962) suggests that the marked discontinuity between
traditional psychoanalytic psychotherapy, with its mutual participation
model, and other help-taking experiences that involve a guidance-cooperation relationship model leads to premature dropouts from traditional
therapy.

For these reasons, rational psychotherapy may have a wider appeal
than many of the traditional techniques. On the other hand, many clients
may experience a feeling of being badgered and set upon if the therapist
is not careful to establish an initially high level of trust and confidence.
It is also somewhat difficult to see how a passive-dependent client could
ever escape his dependency when the therapist is so frankly and openly
a take-charge person. That is, clients may not always respond to what a
therapist verbalizes but to how he verbalizes it. Thus the rational therapist might rigorously attack the irrationality underlying a passive-dependent individual and still do no more than reinforce the sense of impotence
the client feels.

CONSTRUCTIVE ALTERNATIVISM

The complexity of the late George A. Kelly's (1955) psychology of
personal constructs cannot be faithfully presented in a brief statement.

Essentially Kelly thought of every human's approaching his life as a kind of scientist who devises theories in order to anticipate outcome in life situations. Actual events test these theories empirically, and those which are not verified should, of course, be rejected in favor of construct: that conform with reality. Unfortunately, many individuals hold firmly to theories about themselves and others that are repeatedly disconfirmed Thus they experience anxiety, guilt, hostility, and, sometimes, aggression from others—depending upon the particular construct or centrality of the construct that is faulty.

Treatment is direct and rational in tone. Clients are not only asked to examine their personal constructs from the standpoint of evidence for their validity, but are encouraged to devise and act in accord with new and more usable constructs. Kelly is one of the few psychologists to cope in a refreshing way with the concept of psychic determination. He proposes that behavior is indeed determined by one's constructs, but, since it is possible to alter one's theories about one's self and others, a new set of determinants can be adduced.

ADLERIAN THERAPY

In contrast to Freud's psychosocial conflict theory, views of the late Alfred Adler (one of Freud's early colleagues who broke away to found his own school) might be termed teleological, or goal-directed, in character. Individuals strive for personal power, superiority, or achievement which will bring recognition. Because of early experiences (of which Adler believed sibling position to be of significant importance), individuals develop particular, coherent life styles or master plans to achieve power or, more likely, to escape feelings of inferiority that exist, if for no other reason, because one is born weak and helpless into a world of adults. Adler rejected the concept that neurotics are ill in a medical sense and asserted that mental disturbance is merely a discriminably more faulty life style.

Adlerian therapy is distinctly educative in character, with the therapist often bluntly but sincerely confronting the client with his invalid goals and faulty techniques for achieving power. (For example, a person may try to achieve power over others by being excessively demanding, dependent, unscrupulous, competitive or any of the other ploys utilized by individuals designated as neurotic.) Since, in the final analysis, achieving security through power is an illusion, the Adlerian therapist strives, often by his own example, to enhance the client's *Gemeinschaft-gefühl* (social feeling, fellow-feeling, or social interest). To be successful, the client must go beyond insight into his failures in developing a functional life style; he must restructure his roles and redirect his energy into channels reflecting social interest.

WILL THERAPY

Another of Freud's early colleagues who split with the master, the late Otto Rank (1945), focused his attention on the birth trauma as the origin of anxiety and on the dependency-independency conflict around the maternal figure as the orienting influence in the lives of all individuals. According to his thought, to be well adjusted one must use his will, or ego strength, to avoid either symbiotic dependence or lonely isolation from others—two extreme ways of resolving the basic conflict.

Rank's will therapy is conceptualized as analogous in some respects to the original birth trauma, but involving an adult client who can exercise control over his life. For this reason, the therapist fixes a time limit on therapy so that the client can prepare for the severing, of the relationship which is symbolic of rebirth. Technique involves focusing on the present and is relational and educative in character.

GESTALT PSYCHOTHERAPY

Gestalt theory and related practices (Perls, Hefferline, and Goodman 1965) is another existential approach that stresses willingness to risk authentic human encounters as the way out of a personal morass. Heightened awareness of multiple events, both in a therapeutic transaction and outside of it (in order to have meaning must be what is said fleshed out by awareness of tone of voice, posture, syntax, and feeling toward the other person), leads the client to be more vividly in touch with himself and his social environment.

The situation is a total Gestalt (and the only reality) that incorporates the individual (the organism), his needs and the environment. One examines behavior in terms of problem-solving: How does the emergent behavior cope with these three aspects of the Gestalt? The therapist endeavors to help the client become more acutely aware of the multiple facets of each situation and to find and make a solution to the problem inherent in it.

There are no abstract problems, but only real situations. Hence therapy begins at the point at which the client asks, At what moment do I begin not to solve this problem? How do I prevent myself? Broadly conceived, therapy is a repetition of these exercises until the client is able to continue on his own. Gestalt therapists regard each therapeutic encounter as unique, but they have developed a taxonomy of moments of interruption for the guidance of the therapist.

NONRATIONAL THERAPY

Primarily identified with Carl A. Whitaker and Thomas P. Malone (1953, 1961), this approach falls at the experiential end of the continuum in its stress on the experience of feeling as against thinking. Influenced by Eastern philosophy, the authors draw on a Buddhist characterization of a mature person as one who chooses correctly without thinking.

The process of psychotherapy is schematized as having five phases: preinterview, presymbolic, symbolic, ending phase, and post interview. The therapist is mainly involved in the middle three phases, with social workers being responsible for inducing the client into a patient status and assisting in the transition back to the community. The middle phases are further subdivided in (1) anamnesis and symbolic casting stages; (2) competitive, regressive, and core stages; and (3) testing and withdrawal stages.

The skill of the therapist lies in his having greater capacity than the client for symbolic experience and unconscious functioning. As therapy progresses, the therapist draws the client further from preoccupation with reality and deeper into a fantasy world in which intense feeling associated with earlier developmental periods can be experienced. The therapist serves as a sibling or parent image. In later stages, the therapist is seen more as he actually is, and the content has a larger component of reality-testing. Re-repression of unconscious fantasies (now rendered functional rather than disruptive through the agency of the relationship with the therapist) is seen as essential to preclude a hyperawareness of dynamics. The well person should simply experience—not ruminate about his experiences.

CONCLUDING NOTE

As can readily be seen from the sample of therapies described, the ingenuity of theories is almost limitless, and the spectrum of psychological treatments is broad. While it is not possible to generalize without some degree of injustice to the various schools, the following diagram may help the reader conceptualize two of the main parameters along which the therapies lie:

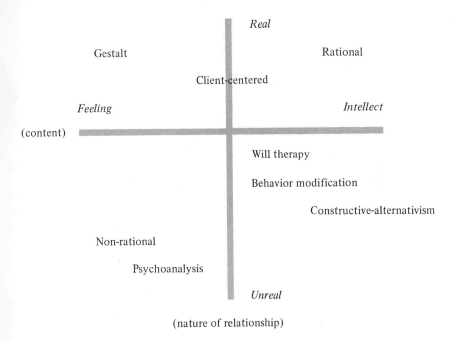

One has to do with the type of content the therapist hopes to elicit in his transactions with his clients(*feeling-intellect,*)and a second having to do with the extent therapy is viewed as an actual valid relationship in contrast to being circumscribed and rather specialized (*real-unreal*) interpersonal experience. A third dimension may be that of therapist activity since therapists who espouse therapy as a real relationship tend to be active and those who view it as significantly different from any ordinary human encounter tend to be passive this additional scale may be unnecessary.

A reader looking at the multiplicity of theories and practices may wonder where the truth lies. The answer is nowhere and everywhere. As noted earlier, many theories and practices grow out of the personal characteristics of the originators. Thus, if therapists in category X are more comfortable being rather cool, rational, and analytic, they will help patients more if they do not try to be warm, active, and spontaneous. Even though techniques and theories may, in part be rationalizations of the originators' personal preferences in interpersonal relations, to the extent that the rationalization promotes a reduction in strain in performing the difficult art of therapy, it serves a useful purpose. After all, none of the therapies described has been tested by scientific standards. The theories and practice are inspired and are deemed valid by both therapists and patients because they work or seem to work. When the methodology suitable to studying psychotherapy scientifically is better developed, one of the findings may be that faithfulness to personal style is an important ingredient in treatment.

This survey of current one-to-one psychotherapies is only a sample of a long list. Moreover, group psychotherapy, which is becoming increasingly prominent as a medium of treatment, has not been covered at all. Most of the schools have revised or extended their theories to cover group procedures, and some new concepts—particularly encounter techniques and sensitivity training—have become very prominent.

It is becoming increasingly difficult in large metropolitan areas, where groups of every description have proliferated, to distinguish between treatment groups, whose goal is change of the individual through therapeutic experience to permit him to pursue life more effectively on his own, and groups in which participation is an end in itself. One person may belong to several groups with overlapping memberships. One is led to speculate that, taken together with dating services, single parties, singles bars, and other sponsored social activities, groups for treatment or merely for "valid" encounters are a new social form that has developed to counteract the isolation of the individual from a more natural and spontaneous social life growing out of family, neighborhood, school, and work groups.

There have been growing indications that a proportion of so-called patients have sought individual as well as group therapy mainly because they lack the support and guidance that comes from membership in and confident acceptance by a social group and therefore are confused, aimless, anxious, and groping for an identity. Since it is man's social affiliations that define him, and since with urbanization and greatly enhanced mobility these have become steadily more tenuous, psychotherapists probably have a discernibly different role than they once had. Whereas the therapist may once have had the job of helping a person more effectively meet his clearly defined and largely inescapable responsibilities, to a particular and limited set of people he now is faced with the problem of providing an anchor for many individuals who for whatever reason lack a dependable, comprehensible affiliation with a durable social group or even with one other person.

This may be one reason why so many superficially different forms of therapy have had apparent success. All of them for a fee, do offer a trustworthy relationship.

References

ALEXANDER, F. *Psychosomatic medicine: Its principles and applications.* New York: W. W. Norton & Co., 1950.

ALLISON, J., BLATT, S. J., & ZIMET, C. N. *The Interpretation of psychological tests.* New York: Harper & Row, 1968.

ANDREWS, J. D. W. Psychotherapy of phobias. *Psychol. Bull.*, 1966, **66**, (6), 455–80.

AULD, F. Emotions in the interview: Can they be measured? *Psychol. Rep.*, 1961, **8**, 239–42.

BARKER, J. C. Behaviour therapy for transvestism: A comparison of pharmacological and electrical aversion techniques. *British J. of Psychia.*, 1965, **111**, 268–76.

BOOMER, D. S. Speech disturbance and body movement in interviews. *J. nerv. ment. Dis.*, 1963, **136**, 263–66.

BORDIN. E. S. Inside the therapeutic hour. In E. A. Rubinstein and M. B. Parloff (Eds.), *Research in psychotherapy.* Washington, D.C.: American Psychological Association, 1959, pp. 235–46.

BRAGINSKY, B. M., & BRAGINSKY, D. D. Schizophrenic patients in the psychiatric interview: An experimental study of their effectiveness at manipulation. *J. consult. Psychol.*, 1967, **31**, 543–47.

BREGER, L., & McGAUGH, J. L. Critique and reformulation of "learning theory" approaches to psychotherapy and neurosis. *Psychol. Bull.*, 1965, **63**, 338–58.

BRUCH, H. *The importance of overweight.* New York: W. W. Norton & Co., 1957.

CARSON, R. C. An introduction to MMPI interpretation. In J. N. Butcher (Ed.), *MMPI: Research developments and clinical applications.* New York: McGraw-Hill Book Co., 1968.

157

Danskin, D. G. Roles played by counselors in their interviews. *J. counsel. Psychol.*, 1955, **2**, 22–27.

Datel, W. E., & Gengerelli, J. A. Reliability of Rorschach interpretations. *J. proj. Tech.*, 1955, **19**, 372–81.

Dent, J. Y. Dealing with the alcoholic at home. *Med. World Lond.*, 1954, **81**, 245.

Draper, E. *Psychiatry and pastoral care.* Englewood Cliffs, N.J.: Prentice-Hall, Inc., 1965.

Dunbar, F. *Emotions and bodily changes.* New York: Columbia University Press, 1954.

Dunlap, K. *Habits, their making and unmaking.* New York: Liveright Publishing Corp., 1932.

Ekman, P. Body position, facial expression, and verbal behavior during interviews. *J. abnorm. soc. Psychol.* 1964, **68**, 295–301.

Ellis, A. Rational psychotherapy. *J. gen. Psychol.*, 1958, **59**, 35–49.

Ellis, A. *Reason and emotion in psychotherapy*, New York: Lyle Stuart, 1962.

Feldman, M. P. Aversion therapy for sexual deviants: A critical review. *Psychol. Bull.*, 1966, **65**, 65–79.

Feldman, M. P., & MacCulloch, M. J. A systematic approach to the treatment of homosexuality by conditioned aversion. Preliminary report. *Amer. J. Psychiat.*, 1964, **121**, 167–72.

Fenichel, O. *The psychoanalytic theory of neurosis.* New York: W. W. Norton & Co., 1945.

Fiedler, F. E. The concept of an ideal therapeutic relationship. *J. consult. Psychol.*, 1950, **14**, 39–45.

Fiedler, F. E. Quantitative studies on the role of therapists' feelings toward their patients. In O. H. Mowere (Ed.), *Psychotherapy: Theory and research.* New York: Ronald Press, 1953, 296–315.

Frank, J. *Persuasion and healing: A comparative study of psychotherapy.* Baltimore, Md.: Johns Hopkins University Press, 1961.

Frank, J. D. The dynamics of the psychotherapeutic relationship. *Psychiat.*, 1959, **22**, 17–39.

Frank, L. K. Projective methods for the study of personality. *J. Psychol.*, 1939, **8**, 389–413.

Frank, L. K. *Projective methods.* Springfield, Ill.: Charles C Thomas, 1948.

Freeman, F. S. *Theory & practice of psychological testing.* New York: Holt, Rinehart and Winston, 1962.

Goffman, E. *The presentation of self in everyday life.* New York: Doubleday & Co., 1961.

Goldstein, A. P., Heller, K., & Sechrest, L. B. *Psychotherapy and the psychology of behavior change.* New York: John Wiley & Sons, 1966.

Gottschalk, L. A., & Auerbach, A. H. *Methods of research in psychotherapy.* New York: Appleton-Century-Crofts, 1966.

Guilford, J. P. A revised structure of intellect. *Reports from the Psychological Laboratory of the University of Southern California*, 1957, No. 19.

GUTHRIE, G. M. Six MMPI diagnostic profile patterns. *J. Psychol.*, 1950, **30**, 317–23.

HALD, J., & JACOBSEN, E. A drug sensitizing the organism to ethyl alcohol. *Lancet,* 1948 (ii), 1001.

HALL, C., & LINDZEY, G. *Theories of personality.* New York: John Wiley & Sons, 1957.

HARROWER-ERICKSON, M. R. Directions for administration of the group test. *Rorschach Res. Exch.,* 1941, **5**, 145–53.

HARROWER-ERICKSON, M. R. A multiple choice test for screening purposes. *Psychosom. Med.,* 1943, **5**, 331–41.

HEINE, R. W. A comparison of patients' reports on psychotherapeutic experience with psychoanalytic, non-directive, and Adlerian therapists. *Psychother.,* 1953, **7**, 16–22.

HOLT, R. R., & LUBORSKY, L. *Personality patterns of psychiatrists.* New York: Basic Books Inc., 1958.

HOLTZMAN, W. H. A brief description of the Holtzman ink blot test. In B. I. Murstein, (Ed.), *Handbook of projective techniques.* New York: Basic Books, Inc., 1965, 417–21.

HOLTZMAN, W. H., & SELLS, S. B. Prediction of flying success by clinical analysis of test protocols. *J. abnorm. soc. Psychol.,* 1954, **49**, 485–98.

HOLTZMAN, W. H., THORPE, J. S., SWARTZ, J. D., & HERRON, E. W. *Inkblot perception and personality.* Austin: University of Texas Press, 1960.

HORNEY, K. *The neurotic personality of our time.* New York: W. W. Norton & Co., 1937.

HORNEY, K. *New ways in psychoanalysis.* New York: W. W. Norton & Co., 1939.

HORNEY, K. *Self analysis.* New York: W. W. Norton & Co., 1942.

HORNEY, K. *Our inner conflicts.* New York: W. W. Norton & Co., 1945.

HORNEY, K. *Neurosis and human growth.* New York: W. W. Norton & Co., 1950.

HOWE, E. S., & POPE, B. Therapist verbal activity level and diagnostic utility of patient verbal responses. *J. consult. Psychol.,* 1962, **26**, 149–55.

KELLY, E. L., & FISKE, D. W. *The prediction of performance in clinical psychology.* Ann Arbor, Michigan: The University of Michigan Press, 1951.

KELLY, G. A. *The psychology of personal constructs.* New York: W. W. Norton & Co., 1955.

KOEGLER, R., & BRILL, N. *Treatment of psychiatric outpatients.* New York: Appleton-Century-Crofts, 1967.

KRASNER, L. The use of generalized reinforcers in psychotherapy research. *Psychol. Rev.,* 1955, **1**, 19–25.

KRASNER, L. Behavior control and social responsibility. *Am. Psychologist,* 1962 (b), **17**, 199–204.

LAMBO, T. A. Patterns of psychiatric care in developing African countries. In Ari Kiev (Ed.), *Magic, faith, and healing.* London: Collier-Macmillan Ltd., 1964.

LAZARUS, A. A. The results of behavior therapy in one hundred and twenty-six cases of severe neurosis. *Behav. Res. Ther.*, 1963, 1, 69–79.

LEVY, D. M. *Studies in sibling rivalry.* New York: The American Orthopsychiatric Association, 1937.

LITTLE, K. B., & SCHNEIDMAN, E. S. The validity of thematic projective technique interpretations. *J. Pers.*, 1955, 23, 285–94.

LOEVINGER, J. Conflict of commitment in clinical research. *Amer. Psychologist*, 1963, 18, 241–51.

LORR, M., KLETT, C. J., & McNAIR, D. M. *Syndromes of psychosis.* New York: The Macmillan Co., 1963.

McNEIL, E. *The quiet furies. Man and disorder.* Englewood Cliffs, N.J.: Prentice-Hall Inc., 1967.

MADDI, S. R. Personality theories: A comparative analysis. Homewood, Ill.: Dorsey Press, 1968.

MALONE, T. P., WITAKER, C. A., WARKENTIN, J., & FELDER, R. E. Rational and nonrational psychotherapy. *Amer. J. Psychother.* 1961, 15, 212–20.

MAY, R. Existence: A new dimension in psychiatry and psychology. In R. May, E. Angel, and H. F. Ellenberger (Eds.), New York: Basic Books, Inc., 1958.

MEEHL, P. E. *Clinical versus statistical prediction.* Minneapolis: University of Minnesota Press, 1954.

MORGAN, C. D., & MURRAY, H. A. A method for investigating fantasies. *Arch. Neurol. Psychiat.*, 1935, 34, 289–306.

MUNROE, R. L. The inspection technique. A modification of the Rorschach method of personality diagnosis for large scale application. *Rorschach Res. Exch.*, 1941, 5, 166–90.

MURRAY, H. A., et al. *Explorations in personality.* New York: Oxford University Press, 1938.

OVERALL, J. E. A configural analysis of psychiatric diagnostic stereotypes. *Behav. Sci.*, 1963, 8, 211–19.

OVERALL, J. E., & GORHAM, D. R. The brief psychiatric rating scale. *Psychol. Rep.*, 1962, 10, 799–812.

PERLS, F., HEFFERLINE, R., & GOODMAN, P. *Gestalt therapy.* New York: Dell Publishing Co., 1965.

PRATT, S., & TOOLEY, J. Contract psychology and the actualizing transactional-field. From *The International Journal of Social Psychiatry* (Congress issue), 1964.

RACHMAN, S. Sexual disorders and behaviour therapy. *Amer. J. Psychiat.* 1961, 118, 235–240.

RACHMAN, S. Current status of behavior therapy. *Arch. gen. Psychiat.*, 1965, 13, 418–23.

RACHMAN, S. Studies in desensitization: I. The separate effects of relaxation and desensitization. *Behav. Res. Ther.*, 1966, 4, 1–6. (a)

RACHMAN, S. Studies in desensitization: III. Speed of generalization. *Behav. Res. Ther.*, 1966, 4, 7–15. (b)

RANK, O. *Will therapy and truth and reality.* New York: Alfred A. Knopf, 1945.

RAPAPORT, D., GILL, M. & SCHAFER, R. *Diagnostic psychological testing.* Chicago: Year Book Medical Publishers, 1945.

RAYMOND, M. J. Case of fetishism treated by aversion therapy. *British Medical J.,* 1956, **2**, 854–57.

RIEFF, P. *The triumph of the therapeutic: Uses of faith after Freud.* New York: Harper & Row, Publishers, 1966.

ROBBINS, L. L. A historical review of classification of behavior disorders and one current perspective. In L. D. Eron (Ed.), *The Classification of Behavior disorders.* Chicago: Aldine Publishing Co., 1966. Pp. 1–37.

ROEN, S. R., OTTENSTEIN, D., ROSENBLUM, G., COOPER, S., & BURNES, A. J. *Communication patterns in community aftercare.* Quincy, Mass.: South Shore Mental Health Center, 1966.

ROGERS, C. R. *On becoming a person.* Boston: Houghton Mifflin Company, 1961.

ROGERS, C. R. *Client-centered therapy.* Boston: Houghton Mifflin Company, 1965.

RORSCHACH, H. *Psychodiagnostics: A diagnostic test based on perception.* New York: Grune & Stratton Inc., 1942.

SARGANT, W., & SLATER, E. *An introduction to physical methods of treatment in psychiatry.* Edinburgh: Livingstone, 1954.

SCHOFIELD, W. *Psychotherapy. The purchase of friendship.* Englewood Cliffs, N.J.: Prentice-Hall, Inc., 1964.

SEEMAN, J. A study of the process of nondirective therapy. *J. consult. Psychol.,* 1949, **13**, 157–68.

SHAKOW, D. The nature of deterioration in schizophrenic conditions. *Nerv. ment. Dis. Monogr.,* 1945 (70), 1–88.

SHAKOW, D. Psychological deficit in schizophrenia. *Behav. Sci.,* 1963, **8**, 275–305.

SHAPIRO, A. K. A contribution to a history of the placebo effect. *Behav. Sci.,* 1960, **5**, 109–35.

SISKIND, G. Fifteen years later: A replication of a semantic study of concepts of clinical psychologists and psychiatrists. *J. Psychol.,* 1967, **65**, 3–7.

SKINNER, B. F. *Science and human behavior.* New York: The Macmillan Company, 1953.

SNYDER, W. U. An investigation of the nature of non-directive psychotherapy. *J. genet. Psychol.,* 1945, **33**, 193–223.

SNYDER, W. U. *The psychotherapy relationship.* New York: The Macmillan Company, 1961.

STRUPP, H. H. Psychotherapeutic technique, professional affiliation, and experience level. *J. consult. Psychol.,* 1955, **19**, 97–102.

STRUPP, H. H. The performance of psychiatrists and psychologists in a therapeutic interview. *J. clin. Psychol.,* 1958, **14**, 219–26.

STRUPP, H. H. Toward an analysis of the psychotherapist's contribution to the treatment process. *Psychiat.,* 1959, **22**, 349–62.

STRUPP, H. H. Psychotherapists in action. New York: Grune & Stratton, 1960. (a)

STRUPP, H. H. Nature of the therapist's contribution to treatment process. *Arch. gen. Psychiat.*, 1960, **3**, 219–31. (b)

SULLIVAN, H. S. *Conceptions of modern psychiatry,* New York: W. W. Norton & Co., 1947.

SULLIVAN, H. S. *The interpersonal theory of psychiatry,* New York: W. W. Norton & Co., 1953.

SULLIVAN, H. S. *The psychiatric interview.* New York: W. W. Norton & Co., 1954.

TERMAN, L. M. *The Measurement of intelligence.* Boston: Houghton Mifflin Company, 1916.

TERMAN, L. M., & MERRILL, M. A. *Measuring intelligence.* Boston: Houghton Mifflin Company, 1937.

WECHSLER, D. *Range of human capacities.* Ed. 2. Baltimore: The Williams & Wilkins Co., 1955.

WECHSLER, D. *The measurement and appraisal of adult intelligence.* Baltimore: The Williams & Wilkins Co., 1958.

WEISS, E., & ENGLISH, O. S. *Psychosomatic medicine: The clinical application of psychopathology to general medical problems.* Philadelphia: W. B. Saunders Co., 1943.

WEPMAN, J. M., & HEINE, R. W. *Concepts of personality.* Chicago: Aldine Publishing Co., 1963.

WHITAKER, C. A., & MALONE, T. P. *The roots of psychotherapy.* New York: Blakiston, 1953.

WITKIN, H. A. Psychological differentiation and forms of pathology. *Journal of Abnormal Psychology,* 1965, **70**, 317–36.

WITKIN, H. A., DYK, R. B., FATERSON, H. F., GOODENOUGH, D. R., & KARP, S. A. *Psychological differentiation.* New York: John Wiley & Sons, 1962.

WITKIN, H. A., LEWIS, H. B., HERTZMAN, M., MACHOVER, K., MEISSNER, P. B., & WAPNER, S. *Personality through perception.* New York: Harper & Row, Publishers, 1954.

WITTENBORN, J. R. The dimensions of psychosis. *J. nerv. Ment. Dis.,* 1962, **134**, 117–28.

WITTMAN, M. P. A scale for measuring prognosis in schizophrenic patients. *Elgin Papers,* 1941, Vol. **4**.

WOLPE, J. *Psychotherapy by reciprocal inhibition.* Stanford: Stanford University Press, 1958.

YARROW, L. J. Maternal deprivation: Toward an empirical and conceptual re-evaluation. *Reviews of research in behavior pathology,* Holmes, D. S. (Ed.). New York: John Wiley & Sons, Inc., 1968, 163–210.

ZIGLER, E., & PHILLIPS, L. Psychiatric diagnosis: A critique. *J. abnorm. soc. Psychol.,* 1961, **63**, 607–18. (a)

ZIGLER, E., & PHILLIPS, L. Psychiatric diagnosis and symptomatology. *J. abnorm. soc. Psychol.,* 1961, **63**, 69–75. (b)

ZUBIN, J. Failures of the Rorschach technique. *J. Proj. Tech.*, 1954, **18**, 303–15.

ZUBIN, J. A biometric model for psychopathology. In R. A. Patton (Ed.), *Current trends in the description and analysis of behavior.* Pittsburgh: University of Pittsburgh Press, 1958.

ZUBIN, J. A biometric approach to diagnosis and prognosis. In J. H. Nodine and J. H. Moyer (Eds.), *Psychosomatic Medicine* (The First Hahneman Symposium). Philadelphia: Lea & Febiger, 1962.

ZUBIN, J. Behavioral concomitants of the mental disorders: A biometric view. In B. Wigdor (Ed.), *Recent advances in the study of behavior change.* Montreal: McGill University Press, 1963.

Index

Cattell, James McKean, 41, 43
Character analysis, 147–48
Character traits, 107
  ego-syntonic, 35
  formation of, 94
Child-rearing practices, 92–97
  behavior modification techniques of, 114
  historical changes in, 89
  inconsistent, 126
Childhood development (see Development)
Classical conditioning, 117
Client-centered (mutual-participation) interviews, 57–58
Client-centered therapy (Rogerian therapy, nondirective therapy), 128–39
  case example of, 137–39
  counselor's role in, 132–34, 139
  principles of, 129–32
  process of, 134–36
  training in, 82, 137
Clinical evaluation, 24–26 (see also Diagnostic procedures; Diagnostic testing)
  function of, 39
  goals of, 25–26
Clinical interviews, 72–73
  as diagnostic tool, 52–58
  participants' roles in, 55–57
  scholastic, 38
  stages of, 142
Cognition (thought), 65, 116–17 (see also Intelligence tests; Memory)
  cognitive development, 116
  cognitive style, 70
  rational approach to, 149
Commitment, 145
Communication, symptoms as form of, 23–24
Community Adaptation Schedule (CAS), 71
Community psychology, 32, 71
Conceptual disorganization, 69
Conditioning, 117–22
  therapeutic, 120–22, 124
Conflict, 48–49, 73–77, 118, 147–48
  dependency-independency, 39, 74, 85, 110–11, 124–26, 137–39, 153
  mental illness caused by, 35
  "real," 147
Congruence, 133, 139
Conscience, 9–11, 13 (see also Superego)
  function of, 9–10
  as interacting subsystem, 16
Conscious, Freudian theory of, 92

Consensual validation, 26, 40, 59–60
  of technical language, 60
Constitutive tests, 45
Constructive alternativism (personal constructs), 32–33, 151–52
Constructive tests, 45
Contract violations, 17–19
Counter-transference, 100
Criterion behavior (problem), 43, 49, 60
Curiosity, 113

Dependence (see also Independence):
  of analysand, 107
  client-centered view of, 131
  dependency-independency conflict, 39, 74, 85, 110–11, 124–26, 137–39, 153
  impotent, 97
Deprivation effects, 114
Desensitization, 80, 120–21
  therapeutic, 120, 125
Destructiveness, dynamics of, 10–12
Development, childhood, 148, 154 (see also Child-rearing practices)
  analysis of, 99–100, 104, 107
  behavioral theory of, 114–16
  client-centered theory of, 131
  neopsychoanalytic view of, 146
  psychosexual, 48, 92–95, 119
Diagnostic procedures, 22–36
  absence of, 132
  diagnostic categories as patterns of reaction, 34
  evolution of, 27–30
  limitations and achievements of, 26–27
  psychological focus of, 31–32
  vocabulary of, 30–31
Diagnostic testing, 24, 36–77
  case example of, 71–77
  development of, 40–44
  methods of, 44–58, 66–70
  training for test administration, 61-62
  utility of, 36–40, 43
Disorientation, 69
Displacement process, 103
Dream analysis, 98
Drives, 84 (see also Gratification; Instinct; Needs; Sex drive)
  basic, 112–13
Dynamics (see Psychodynamic assessment; Psychodynamic theories)
Dysfunction, dynamics of, 10–13

Ego, 90–92, 95–98, 148
  function of, 91–92

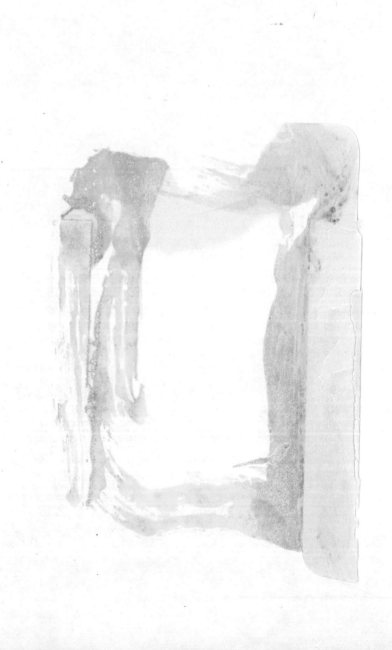